Gems of Growth

Gems of Growth

A Personal Story of Growing Up,
Growing Apart, and Growing Into
Who You Were Meant to Be

LINE SAND

Publisher: BoD · Books on Demand, Strandvejen 100, 2900 Hellerup, bod@bod.dk

Print: Libri Plureos GmbH, Friedensallee 273, 22763 Hamborg, Germany

Cover Design: © Rebeka Vařáková
Photo: © Caroline Hebbelstrup

ISBN: 978-87-7170-023-7

DEDICATIONS

To my grandma, whom I never got to know, but who sparked my love for stories from an early age.

To my family, who introduced me to a life of faith in God.

To Michael for telling me that now was the time for me to write.

To Esti for telling me that there was a story unfolding in my life with new pages added every day that would someday make up a book.

To Sarah for being a constant friend through all the ups and downs in this story.

To everyone who reads about themself in the pages of this story, because their path at some point intertwined with mine. I am truly grateful for all the memories, all the encouragement, and all the lessons.

To God, in the hope that You will use my story in Your plans for people, just like I have been blessed by reading the stories of other people.

CONTENTS

INTRODUCTION
January 2025

This story is a story about growth. Not that I will claim myself to be an expert on growth. Rather, I think that I will leave my story here for you to read, and then I hope you will be able to derive your own takeaways on growth, because that is just the thing, isn't it? Growth, when it comes to personal and spiritual growth, is not of a substance which allows us to easily measure, compare, or even encapsulate it in a description of what it looks like.

Growth does not look like that perfect linear graph by which we depict financial or physical growth processes. Nor does it look like reaching a destination, which is otherwise implied in the terms *growing up* or *growing into something.* Growth is a fact of life, and it is unavoidable. It is deeply personal and yet universal. Growth is messy and unpredictable, sometimes manifesting itself in huge, sudden leaps while other times stagnating for years. Growth is two steps forward and one step back, and it is going around in circles in the desert for years, before you see what God was doing all along. Growth is rarely experienced in the day-to-day moments of our lives, but looking back, we might recognize that growth happened. Growth is best captured over the long term, and as I went through my journals, reading page after page of my well-documented coming-of-age narrative, I realized that it was a story of growth. I wrote this book from the entries of my journals, in which I poured out my heart and soul trying to make sense of my journey as it unfolded.

I don't know where you find yourself in your growth journey, but it is my sincere hope that my story will provide you with comfort, peace, and hope in the different seasons of your life. Most of all, I hope it will inspire you to find God at work in your own life. He is truly faithful, and you can trust Him with your life journey.

With love, Line

THE INVITATION
December 2012

On a random Wednesday in the 8th grade, I did something terrible. I denied my faith in Jesus. The way it happened was that one of my classmates started talking about faith and church. Because his parents knew my family a little bit, he started asking all kinds of questions like "*doesn't your family go to church quite a lot, Line?*" and "*aren't your family like real believers?*" Being religious was not a cool thing at my school, so I always kept very quiet about the fact that I already knew the stories from the Bible that we were taught in our religion classes, or why I could never come play with my friends on Sundays before lunch. My parents wanted for me and my sisters to go to a public school, because they didn't want to shield us too much from the world in which we were going to grow up, and I have an immense respect for that decision today. When I was in the middle of it though, I often wished that my family looked more like other families, and that we didn't have this odd lifestyle that set me apart from the other kids in school. I wanted to fit in and feel accepted, but our weekly church services and saying grace before dinner felt like threats to my maintaining that. So, when I was suddenly called out by this guy in the middle of the classroom, I panicked and knew no other way to save face than to deny it all blankly.

The bad conscience hit me like a tidal wave, immediately and with full force. I had denied my faith. I remembered the story from the Bible of Peter denying his being a disciple of Jesus, and I felt that this was really bad. Not only was it lying, but it was lying about my family's association with Christ. I felt guilty and needed to confess to someone, so I wrote a text to one of my girlfriends in class, who had been around when it happened. She comforted me by making sure I knew that she didn't find me odd, and she told me that it was nobody's business whether my family were believers or not. This, however, did not completely remove the guilt, because I knew we were supposed to share our faith with others, not keep it a secret.

I came home from school that day and found a letter addressed to me. It was a letter of admission to a Christian boarding school, and it made me beyond happy to be granted this amazing opportunity. Little did I know at the time that this was a real "You're a wizard, Harry"-moment for me. I had always felt odd and out of place in my childhood social spheres due to my Christian inheritance, but this letter marked an invitation to embark on the wildest journey of discovering a whole new world of what it meant to be a believer in Jesus. Just like Harry Potter went to Hogwarts, I would be going to this school and find out that I was not odd - just built for a different life. I would be learning, growing, and discovering among peers, who were on a similar trajectory in life, and I would fit right in. To this day, I can almost hear God speak the words "You're mine, Line" over the moment when I opened my letter of admission. I had denied Him earlier that day, because I did in fact not know Him, but He responded with a loving invitation for me to come closer and get to know Him better.

LONGING FOR MORE
October 2013

Boarding school was in many ways a dream come true for me, but there was one thing bothering me in this Christian social bubble. I noticed that some of the other teens had something that I didn't. It seemed that they enjoyed another level of intimacy with God, where they not only prayed to Him, but also had deeply personal encounters with Him. I longed for this level of intimacy in my own relationship with God, and I asked Him for it, but nothing really seemed to happen. I began to wonder if I was doing something wrong, since I couldn't hear Him or experience Him in the same way other people did, and in October it culminated in me crying out in frustration in front of my contact teacher at the school.

My contact teacher was one of those people, who listened well without saying a lot. It was a good strategy on a 15-year-old girl, who needed plenty of time to reflect and often found it challenging to put into words everything that was happening on the inside. This time was no different. Only after a long time, he broke the silence and shared with me something that I have remembered ever since. He said, "*you see, we don't always get the answer to why God holds something back from us that we ask of Him, but being in a place of longing for more of Him is the best place to be, and you can be absolutely certain that He delights in that.*"

Sometimes we get impatient with the processes of life, and we want growth to happen faster than it does. But maybe growth is more often the slow and steady long-term steps than it is the big immediate leaps. I guess God knows what He is doing by leading us the long way through to our destinations.

GROWING UP
March 2015

My second year of boarding school was marked by challenges of different kinds. As the second school year began, and all the new students settled in around me, I found it incredibly difficult to connect with people, and I ended up having only a small group of friends around me. These people became my lifeline, and the friendships went deep by all the time we spent together. For that reason, it completely broke my heart when one of "my" people stopped at the school around Christmas and only chose to tell me a few days before he went home. It felt like he had not only left the school but me as well, and I missed him every day for a long time.

Around that time, we changed dorm rooms at the school, and I wasn't too happy with my new roomies. They were all very alike with their black, white, and grey décor, and I felt out of place with my bright pink blanket and my yellow stuffed duckling. They were rude towards our teachers, they were very much into their looks, and they spoke about boys, clothes, and bodies in a way I couldn't' relate to. We had been allowed to wish for roomies, and while they had all wished for each other, I had been granted none of my wishes. I felt overlooked by our teachers, and I was tired of always being disregarded, because I was known as the easy-going kid, who could fit in everywhere or be a good influence on anyone. I wanted for once to have someone take my wishes and wants into account as well.

In March my two best friends at the school started dating. All three of us had been very close and spent almost all our time together, laughing, joking, and having amazing, deep talks, and now suddenly I could tell that I was being left out. I wouldn't admit to them how much it hurt me. It was not like they did anything wrong, so I knew that it was just my own problem to deal with, and I didn't want to lose more of my best friends. The pain was still there, however, and at some point, it had stored up in such measures that it no longer fit inside of me. When I didn't let it out of my mouth directly, it spilled out in the form of sarcastic comments that I hoped would be disguised as humor. Sadly, though, I didn't manage to fool them, and one day they both added to my hurt by telling me that they thought I had become very mean lately. It took a long time for me to find my way in our friendship and adjust to the fact that I had to let go of the three-musketeers-friendship I had enjoyed so much.

This year, for the first time in my life, I was also faced with deeper insecurities about my looks. Growing up, it never took up much space in my friendships, but just like Adam and Eve in the Garden of Eden suddenly had their innocence disrupted by the discovery that they were naked, it felt like a certain way of self-criticism was suddenly planted in my head. Over time, it gained more ground by feeding on the experiences I had throughout that year. Low self-esteem was a common problem among the girls I spent time with, and now, when my best male friend chose our other friend over me, I couldn't help but compare myself to her. What had made him fall for her and not for me? What was I missing to have someone find me attractive? Would I have to make more of an effort? Did I even have what it would take or was I just not girlfriend material?

It felt like the combined experiences of that second school year rid me of my innocent outlook on the world. The last pieces of the simplicity of childhood were slowly dissolving, and I was now left to face adulthood with all its complexity, insecurity, and responsibility. As much as I wanted to, there was no turning back. I was growing up.

TWO WORLDS
May 2016

For me, starting gymnasium meant that I would once again join paths with some of the people I grew up with. Although not much had changed on the outside, I felt like a completely different person from who I had been only two years prior, and I wondered if it would be difficult for me to reconnect with all of them. Would it show that Jesus had altered the foundation of my life? I kind of hoped that it would, and at the same time I feared losing friendships that I valued. What actually happened during my first year in gymnasium, though, was… nothing. When you get a heart transplant, others don't necessarily notice unless they either get really close to you or they find out because you tell them. Since I last saw my friends, Jesus had given me a new heart, and He was now in charge of all the whys of my actions, but my behavior in general hadn't changed radically enough for anyone of my old friends to notice the change of heart. They didn't get close enough to see it, and I was reluctant to initiate such deep levels of conversation. Sometimes I wondered if they ever even went to the levels of sharing core beliefs with anyone.

In one area, though, I stood out to my friends. I never learned how to navigate the heavy drinking culture, which I discovered to be one of the core building blocks of gymnasium social life. The very first party became my very last one as well, because the experience was nothing less than horrifying. As a non-drinker, I couldn't find my place in a setting where all activities were built up around consuming as much alcohol as possible. I observed with dismay how the five guys in our class, whom none of the girls would ever consider in broad daylight, suddenly became the objects of rivalry for cheap attention and admiration at these parties. And with absolute disgust, I found myself way too easily being swayed into the same pattern of chasing cheap flatter. As I didn't like neither the atmosphere of these parties, nor myself when I participated in them, I chose to just not go. Although I did miss out on a lot and sometimes found the social structures in class having changed due to events of a weekend party, I was okay. I found in my class a group of girls, who also enjoyed slumber parties, board game evenings, and amusement parks, and the memories I created with these girls throughout my time in gymnasium became absolute treasures to me.

When I turned 18, I threw a big party for a bunch of my friends from boarding school and after much dread and consideration of mixing people from what felt like two different worlds, I decided to invite two girls from my class as well. To my big surprise they blended in well with my boarding school friend group, and we all ended up having an amazing and fun night together. A few weeks later, one of the girls came to me and expressed how truly unique it had been for her to observe the friendships we all shared. She had spent a year at a boarding school as well but in her words, she would have never been able to gather her friends like that, boys and girls, and been able to just enjoy each other's company without sexual tensions, drama, or alcohol involved. I think what she saw that night was what Jesus does to a community of people, and I wish that I would have mixed up my two worlds a little bit more often for my non-believing friends to join in and enjoy the special unity among my church friends. Who knows, - maybe they would have picked up the scent of Jesus along the way?

A LATE-NIGHT WALK
October 2017

I liked a guy from church. He was intelligent, good-looking, and he came from a family with values like those of my own. I wanted to get to know him better, but I was way too shy and self-conscious to make much of an effort. That's what usually happened when I started liking someone, and maybe that's why, at the age of 19, my only experience with romance was one-sided crushes. But something was different this time. During the past half year, there had been small signs that would indicate that he might have taken an interest in me, as well. The signs were not clear though, and I wavered back and forth in all the insecurity of whether he liked me or not.

In October, we went to church camp, and on the last night most of the youth group loaded up the cars and went to McDonald's. I was tired and just wanted to go to bed. To my surprise, he stayed back as well, and when we had to turn our separate ways for the night, I could tell he was hesitating a little bit, but I didn't give it more thought. I went to my room, changed into my pajamas, and checked my phone one last time before going to bed, and my phone lit up with a message from him! Long story short, we went for a walk around town at 3 o'clock in the night, and I was so overwhelmed by it all that I was way too shy to properly keep a conversation going.

In the following days, we wrote back and forth a little bit, and I enjoyed the witty bantering and the feeling of something new and exciting being just around the corner. But then time went by, and when he never initiated a second date, I began to wonder if the first one should even be considered a date. Confused and insecure, I decided to just tell him how I felt. Only after way too long, he replied that he had had some doubts after our talk, but that I seemed like a sweet girl and that he really didn't want to hurt me. How much time and pain it would have spared me to have realized already then that when a guy tells you that he doesn't want to hurt you, it's a sure sign that he doesn't want to be the one to make you happy either. He let me know that he wanted to get to know me better without steering our relationship in any specific direction, and probably without his intend, and because he didn't want to hurt me, he unwisely left the door on hold - a door I would not be able to shut completely close again for several years.

CAREER CHOICES
March 2018

When I was growing up, I was a very creative kid. I made tons of drawings, and all the books of wonderful stories I read served as inspiration for my art. I drew everything I dreamt of doing and experiencing, and I had beautiful, big dreams for my life. If you would have asked me what I wanted to be when I grew up, you would have heard me mention things like a designer, an architect, or a decorator. I loved to express myself through fashion and art, and I spent hours and hours on creating. In my teen years, I was a big fan of Taylor Swift (I still admire her to this day), because she seemed to represent everything, I aspired to become. I was mesmerized with her storytelling, and the way she would use all her experiences, good and bad, and turn them into beautiful art for other people to relate to. I knew I also wanted to be a person, who would create beautiful things for other people to admire and be blessed by.

At some point, though, I buried my artistic dreams in the name of growing up. The thing about big dreams is that they often seem unattainable or at least, the path towards fulfilling them is one paved with uncertainty and risk. So when the time came for me to take active steps towards my future, I traded off uncertainty and risk for feasibility and safety. Whereas my fellow students all made time for one or more sabbath years to have fun, travel the world, and take a break from the straight path of education in front of us, I felt no need for a break and decided to just continue with my studies right away. I went for a business degree at the university in a mid-sized city close to the small town where I grew up. Studying business wasn't something I had ever considered previously in my life, but it seemed like a certain way to find a steady, well-paid job later on, which was reason enough for me. The decision of attending university and aim for a degree was applauded in my head by various of my former teachers, who had urged me to make good use of the talents I had been given.

Somehow, I had convincingly persuaded myself that the very big dreams of my heart were out of reach, and therefore I could feel comfortable aiming for a good, steady job, a family of my own, and serving in church.

Without noticing, I built a nice little box for my aspirations in life and told myself that the goals within the frames of this box, were everything I wanted and needed. In other words, without my realizing it, I settled.

MOVING OUT
August 2018

One of the things I was really looking forward to in my new season was moving out on my own. I had found an adorable little studio apartment that came with everything I needed, and with a lot of consideration and care, I decorated it into a home. I was beyond happy to finally have my own place with my own routines and complete freedom to do things my way, and I was somewhat relieved to leave my childhood home behind.

I had stood on the sideline, watching my mom battle depression throughout all of my teenage years. She is one of the strongest and bravest people I know, and there is no way, I can ever know how much strength it took for her to just get through another day, but I did experience the cracks and bruises that this ugly disease unmistakably left on our home. Depression sucks out all the life and joy of a house and leaves behind only a nasty, weary silence that you at all costs try not to break, so it leaves you walking around on eggshells. I longed for a place that would allow me freedom, spontaneity, and hospitality, so as I decorated my little home with furniture, kitchenware, and pictures, I also filled the place with dreams of friends, cookouts, late-night conversations, and moments of worship and prayer.

After my first day in the apartment, I was astonished by the silence. But it wasn't a silence like the one at my childhood home. This silence was peaceful, and I felt content as I spent the last weeks of summer exploring my new neighborhood and enjoying the floods of dreams and possibilities that often accompany these types of new beginnings.

"CAN YOU DELIVER TO UNI?"
October 2018

I find it fascinating, how the small choices we make in the glimpse of a moment can sometimes have such an impact on our lives in the long run. On my very first day at the university, I walked into a classroom of 130 people I didn't know and found an empty seat next to two girls, who looked approachable. We started talking, and one of those girls became my very good friend and favorite study-buddy throughout all five years of my education.

I have often wondered what would have happened if I had chosen to sit next to some other people that day? Would everything have played out differently? It's a no-brainer to me that this girl was a blessing from God, but how did that friendship come about by such a seemingly random decision? It makes me wonder how much God actively has His hand in the small and seemingly insignificant actions of our days, but it also leaves me in awe to think of how many different trajectories God chose to work with, when He decided to give us a free will and left up to us all the small decisions that generates a million different outcomes.

I loved my new life as a university student. I loved the freedom and the flexibility of going to classes and spending most of my time studying on my own. Organization and business were completely new fields to me, and it suddenly required much more of me than my earlier years of education did, but I gladly gave it everything I had. I had always been eager to learn and in this season, I loved expanding my world by lengths as I deep-dived into books on organizational theory, accounting practices, and statistics. My new friend and I spent a lot of our time studying together, and sometimes we joined forces with more of our fellow students. In October, when we had a big math assignment coming up, we pulled a late-nighter and ordered pizza to be delivered to the university, and I remember thinking how blessed I was in this season of my life to have the freedom of answering to no one and do spontaneous math-and-pizza dates with great people on a random weekday.

BAPTISM
March 2019

Something had been rumbling in my mind during the past few months. Should I get baptized? As it was common practice in the Pentecostal movement where I grew up, I had been blessed, not baptized as an infant, and it was now my own decision if I wanted to get baptized and when. I had studied how baptism was the practice in the stories of the Bible and honestly, I found it incredibly difficult to see how it applied to me today. I was completely on board with it being a public declaration of faith, but it was the mysterious water part that I couldn't quite come to terms with.

For five years now, I had been following Jesus as my Lord and Savior, and to me it seemed odd that I would only now go through the ritual that marks the death of the old life and the beginning of a new one. Wouldn't that invalidate the last five years of my life, somehow? If baptism in water was such a vital part of one's salvation, how would I explain the growth and acts of God in my life up until now? Further, I couldn't even tell much of a difference between life before my decision of following Him and after. I didn't have that story of repentance from a horrible life that changed in a moment when I surrendered myself to Jesus. It rather felt like He had always been there in my life and had only grown bigger and been allowed to take more ownership over time. I knew, however, that Jesus had lived a perfect, sinless life in relationship with His Father, but He was still baptized as an adult to somehow lead the way for the rest of his disciples.

Even though I didn't get satisfactory answers to all my questions about the ritual, I decided to go ahead and get baptized in March. I knew I wanted to follow Jesus' example with my life, and if the next step was to follow Him into the baptismal grave, then that was what I was going to do. I would lean into the mystery that unarguably comes with being led by a transcendent God, and I wanted to take steps of obedience before fully seeing and knowing in my own limited understanding.

As I went into the water that day in March, I remember thinking "*this is for you, Jesus!*" and as I got out of the water, it felt as though God was speaking over me, words similar to those He spoke over Jesus: "*You are my beloved daughter, and I am well pleased with you.*"

THE GENDARME PATH
August 2019

My friend and I just walked 84 kilometers in two and a half days' time. We went hiking on a beautiful coastal trail in the southern part of Denmark, and we were excited for the challenge as well as for having this experience together. The first day was amazing, emersed with energy, great talks, and taking in the views along the route. On the second day, however, things got a little heavier. We were such amateurs that we didn't consider the strain on our legs and feet by walking for an entire day without any training for it. We just went from 0 to 100 and were completely taken by surprise when a night of rest did not take away the soreness in our bodies. The last one and a half days of walking were painful, and it was interesting to observe what happened to us. The conversation died out, and we walked in silence. We ate mackerel in tomato out of a can for breakfast, and we didn't even care. All the things that had been taking up space in my mind before the trip slipped into the background and only my most basic needs became important. It's hard to understand now, but we almost gave up 18 kilometers before we hit the finish line, because we were out of food and couldn't even handle the thought of walking extra precious kilometers to stock up on our food supplies for another day. We mustered enough energy, however, to just power through and close the last distance of the hike on that same day. Those last hours were completely silent as both of us focused all of our energy into placing one foot in front of the other to keep the pace. There was no capacity for talking, whatsoever, but as soon as we crossed the finish line that evening, all the adrenaline and joy of conquering the challenge, gave us back the ability to laugh and joke about what complete idiots we were.

I was never one for doing stupid, crazy things in my life, but this experience made me feel alive, somehow. I had pushed my physical boundaries to the limits, and it was fun to see what happened to my priorities when putting myself under this amount of pressure. I guess sometimes it's good for us to place ourselves outside of our comfort zones and look at life from a little bit of a different angle. That's how we learn more about ourselves, and discover opportunities for growth.

WHEN TRUTH SETS YOU FREE
May 2020

Why on earth didn't I do this a long, long time ago? was the slightly rebuking question, I asked myself when I had finally mustered the courage to gain closure by telling the guy from my late-night-walk that I still liked him after two and a half years of passively waiting around. He let me down gently, but with all the clarity our previous conversations had lacked, and I was left with being mad at myself for having spent so much time entangling myself in hopes and dreams that had no roots in reality.

In the days after our conversation, I was surprised by how quickly I was feeling okay again. Of course I was disappointed, but at the same time I had been so exhausted by the whole situation that somehow, the closure was all I needed to feel at peace again. Though a part of me felt the hurt and shame of getting a rejection from a guy I really liked, I was generally proud of myself for bravely standing up for my feelings and my needs - even though I did it two and a half years later than many other people would have. I didn't realize it at the time, but what I felt was freedom. I had allowed all my hopes and dreams of my future to be shaped and limited by the hopes of a future relationship with this guy, and now that I finally let go of that one dream, it pulled a plug that made all the connected dreams come tumbling down as well. The walls of this neat little box of contentment that I had built up around myself were destroyed, leaving me gazing at wider horizons in every direction.
That day, I promised myself that I would never again wait for so long to gain clarity in any relationship, and then I asked God to fill the void in me with new dreams.

A few days later at a youth gathering, I received a word from God that He was in the process of doing a great work in me, and that it would feel very much like deep waters. This was indeed the starting point of a journey, where God would take me deeper and further than I would've ever imagined at the time. Like you would replant a tree out of a small pot to allow it room for further growth, I had finally let go of what didn't fit into my life anymore so I could make room for all that Jesus would have for me in the future, and I found such joy in dreaming bigger dreams with Him in all areas of my life.

NORWAY GETAWAY
August 2020

I fully enjoyed my newfound freedom, and in August, I packed my parents' old tent into my car, picked up two of my best friends, and went on a spontaneous three-day trip to Norway. I had been a little nervous about this trip, because I had never done anything like it before. Would we be okay by just going with a tent and my car? We had nothing planned beforehand but would just try to figure it all out along the way.

After one rainy night in Kristiansand, we chose to drive directly north and after looking at a few different sites, we chose to set up the tent on a gorgeous, primitive campsite next to a beautiful lake. The next day, we went on a long hike to a mountainside view post that fully took my breath away, and when we came back in the evening, tired and with sunkissed cheeks, we made dinner on a gas burner, played cards, laughed A LOT, and had great talks about our lives and dreams of the future.

When we left to drive south again the next day, we noticed that the camp site would close for the season on that exact same day, and we praised God for the timing of our stay. It had been wonderful to wake up in the morning with a post card view towards lake, trees, and mountains and compared to the other more elaborate and luxurious camp sites we had passed on our way, this place felt like a little hidden gem, that perfectly matched our preferences. It had been a gift from a good Father, who knew us all very well.

From the ferry on the way home, we watched the most beautiful sunset, and I stood there thinking about how this trip had satisfied a deep longing inside of me. It had been a wonderful three-day adventure of exploring and fully living life in the present, and God had been incredibly faithful in showing up, leading the way, and He had even made sure to exceed our expectations. I knew I wanted my life to look more like this in general. To be always on adventure with God alongside great people, letting go of the planning and controlling outcomes. To just lean back and let happen, trusting that my Heavenly Father knows me well enough to fill my life with all the things that touches my heart in a special way.

PROVINSIAL PRESSURE
September 2020

While God was altering and expanding my dreams and aspirations for life on the inside of me, nothing really changed on the outside. My weekly schedule was still occupied with business studies, my job in sales at a local company, and my role of being a leader team member in our youth group. Maybe this was why, when a new guy joined our youth group, almost all my friends tried to pair us up, and I could see why they would think it was a great match.

He was intelligent, good-looking, family-oriented, and had flair for business as well. He was completely the image of the guy I always thought I would end up with some day. The problem was, however, that what I had wanted for so long was now being drastically altered. I knew I wanted more of God in my life, and it had implications on everything else, including what qualities I would be looking for in a potential future spouse. When all my friends tried to make this match happen, it made me feel like they tried to push me back into a box I had finally been able to escape from. I wasn't planning on going back, but how fragile was this change of heart, if even my best friends didn't notice it? I desperately wanted them to be cheering me on - not holding me back.

But how do you explain to your loved ones that the best intentions they have on your behalf are simply not enough for you without coming off as an arrogant prat? How do you tell them that the thought of living a life similar to theirs, would now make you feel like you were settling, somehow? For the first time, I was introduced to a very specific kind of loneliness — the kind that accompanies stepping out on a journey that not everyone can follow, let alone understand. I knew that Jesus required of his followers, the willingness to leave behind what was needed in order to follow Him, and even though it felt scary and lonely for me to leave some people behind on the shore, I wanted to trust Him for His provision out there on the depths ahead of me.

LEADER IN THE MAKING
October 2020

O ver the course of my bachelor's degree, I had been introduced to a variety of different aspects of business, and as much as I had enjoyed expanding my knowledge within every single course, I found my favorite topics to be within the range of leadership and organization. I had been back and forth between a master's degree in either Business Intelligence or Organization and Leadership, but as I progressed in the final semesters of my bachelor's program, I was more and more set on specializing in the "softer" aspects of business. Where my fellow students applied the theories of these courses to the business world, however, I primarily dreamt about using my knowledge to build the church.

My heart for church had grown bigger over the last few years, and this fall my role as a youth leader granted me the opportunity to grow in my leadership skills. As I gained more responsibility in taking care of our youth group in all its diversity, my pastoral heart grew bigger, and so did the challenges I faced in relation to the people, I was leading. My pastor used to say that working with people is a hassle, and within these months, I began to see what he meant. It was worth it, though, and the dream of doing ministry slowly took up a more central role in my dreams of the future. *A few things lead me in the direction of believing that God might have plans for me to be a pastor's wife in the future*, was what I wrote down in my journal one day as God put on my heart a vision of me and my future husband, ministering together. I didn't know exactly what it would look like or what to do with it, but I wanted to trust for Jesus to lead the way in that. For now, I was content with dreaming big dreams about my future and take on the challenge of growing my leadership skills and my love for people.

GROWING ROOTS

January 2021

My life had been a little bit too loud lately, and I didn't like it. I always had several things going on at the same time. I couldn't watch a movie without scrolling on my phone. I never made food without having some TV show running in the background. I never read without listening to music. There were too many inputs all the time, and I wanted to bring back the simplicity of living life without constant noise.

That's why, when Covid-19 once again threw the whole country into lock-down, I decided that I might as well make the best of it, so I began the new year with a fast from streaming services and social media. In the absence of these time thieves, I got to read a lot, and one book by Magnus Malm hit me right in the core of my heart. Throughout the pages of the book, he wrote so profoundly of the most important things in life and how our deeply personal relationship with God should never be exceeded by our public ministries. I knew I had to make these truths my own somehow, so I wrote down the key takeaways of every chapter and rewrote them into prayers to pray over my life. Just as much as I sensed that God was calling me into something great, I knew that right now He was teaching me essentials. A tree is only as strong as its roots, and it takes lots of time hidden away to grow roots strong enough to make way for a healthy and fruitful tree. I knew this time of lock-down was a time where He wanted me to fully focus on me and Him. Instead of coming to Him for help with the people I served at church or the next sermon I was going to prepare, He invited me to get to know Him on His terms and for the sake of enjoying Him alone.

HEROES OF FAITH
February 2021

My youth pastor and his family lived just across the street from me, and I loved how they invited me into their family life with open arms. On one evening in February, they invited me over to watch that day's teaching of a prophetic 5-day challenge, we were all doing. I was simultaneously amazed and frustrated with the teaching, because this guy on the screen talked about our relationship with God as something so natural and so intimate that it looked like nothing I knew from my own experience. I had tons of questions about moving in the prophetic and hearing God's voice, and my youth pastor and his wife were happy to help me process all of it.

This particular evening was representative of their entire ministry, when I think about it. Time and time again, I would see them open up their home, their schedule, and their hearts to disciple me and the other young people in our church. They would answer our questions, give us advice, and walk the extra mile for us, when we needed it most. They invited us close enough to see lives that were authentically lived, and when life got messy, we saw a faith that stood strong. Only a few months ago, they had gone through the process of losing their newborn child, and at the memorial service, when there was a time for worship, I watched my youth pastor being the first one in the room to stand to his feet, lift his hands, and proclaim the goodness of God. That made a tremendous mark on me - not the action in itself, but because I had been close enough throughout the whole process to see that his faith was a rock solid one that hadn't wavered under an incredible weight of crisis, hurt, and sorrow.

Role models are important to all of us, especially in the crazy years of growing up and finding our way in the world, and in my humble opinion, people like my youth pastor and his wife are far too rare nowadays. I consider myself incredibly blessed to have journeyed so close with them for a season in my life, and I pray that I will be able to pass that on to someone else one day.

FRIENDSHIP SORROW
April 2021

I never considered myself the person to put many demands on my friends. On the contrary, I was that very easy-going friend, who would let you take part in my life in any way that would fit the best with you. But lately, something had changed a little, and I wasn't too happy about it. Maybe it was because I already felt a general pattern of losing connections due to the drastic changes that were going on inside of me. It seemed to me that genuine friendships became harder to find, so when I found it in a girl from church, I was beyond thrilled. We could share faith, dream big dreams about the future, and it seemed that we preferred each other's company, so it weighed incredibly heavy on me when she started dating a guy from church only a few months later.

There is this sorrow that kicks in when another one of your friends get into a relationship. It's not jealousy exactly, but it is that feeling of having to step aside to make space for that person in their life. It's the sadness of letting go of much-valued time and attention that was yours when you were both single. I was not looking for a relationship myself, but I still longed to be put first by the people I would put first. It felt incredibly selfish for me to deny her the very thing, we both so deeply longed for, only because I wanted her to myself right now, but as I watched my friend enter a new season that changed her priorities, I couldn't help but mourn the loss of something I only got to have for a very short time.

NEW ADVENTURES
June 2021

In the last couple of months, I had felt a growing restlessness within. I thought it had to do with the fact that as I approached the end of my bachelor's studies, I was looking into two more years on the master's program that would look very similar to my last three years. The only difference would be that I had recently moved into a bigger apartment, and I would now have to commute to a larger city for my lectures and exams. I was afraid to admit it, but the prospect of two more years like this bored me. I longed for greater adventures with Jesus, but I didn't know what to change in my life to get there.

Then, one night at the end of June, something completely unexpected happened. Only on that same day I had wrapped up the very last part of my bachelor's degree by presenting my thesis to the company with whom we collaborated, and then in the evening, I went to a service in my church. I came without any big expectations but to pray for other people, as I had been asked to join the prayer team for the night.

During the evening, I moved down to the back of the room to ask the Holy Spirit what He wanted to do through me, and then something happened inside of me that I couldn't really explain. I just knew that I cast a look to a window frame, where we kept different brochures, and a very specific one caught my attention. It was a pamphlet on a church leadership program, and in that moment, I just knew deep down that God wanted me to adjust my plans, and that He invited me to do this program and follow Him further into the direction of ministry. I felt completely overwhelmed and cried for the rest of the night, making my church family think that something was all wrong, but I just couldn't help it.

The next few days were a combination of crazy excitement about the new things God was calling me into and a fear of the unknown. I had to find out exactly how I would be able to do this program. The more I thought about it, the more attractive it became for me to cancel my master's studies, find a job instead, and spend more time in church. There was one problem, however. The apartment I moved into just two weeks prior, was one of those I could only be living in, if I would continue with my university studies. There was a lot of uncertainty connected to finding a new home and a job. I had a tough conversation with my parents, and their concerns about my change of direction left me feeling discouraged and all alone.

As I shared my decision with more and more people, I was hit by bigger waves of fear, and one night it consumed me so much that I went to bed early and tried to just sleep through it. As I lay in bed, though, I had a full on panic attack, and it felt like I was being physically strangled. In that moment I didn't even care if I was bothering anyone, - I just knew that I couldn't be alone, so I grabbed my phone and wrote to my youth pastor's wife, and she immediately came over. She spoke truth over my situation, and it calmed me down. This was the "realizing the storm and waves" moment that comes with all big leaps of faith. My spirit had been quick to accept God's invitation, but now the consequences of the decision caught up. Would I have to move again? Where would I then live? Could I find a part-time job? Would I have to quit my student job? Would I regret not doing my master's studies? We prayed together, and I slept peacefully through the night, but the next day, fear quickly crept back in, and my mind was working overtime, trying to find the best way through. Later that day a text from my youth pastor's wife made all the puzzle pieces fall into place. *Would it be possible for me to do my master's studies and this church leadership program at the same time?* Here was the solution. This way I could stay in my new home, and I would be able to do all the things I wanted to do.

I knew it was going to be two very busy years with master studies, theology studies, job, church, family, and friends, but this was the solution that brought me peace, and even though several people expressed their concerns about me taking on so much, I optimistically sticked to my decision.

SAHARA SARAH
July 2021

Everyone should have a friend like this in their life - one of those friends who knows how to make an adventure out of every mundane moment, and someone who breaks up your daily routine by randomly showing up at your front door.

This was one of my best friends - and is still to this day. She grew up in Africa, and she was a badass motorcross driver, who knew how to draw me out of my shell. Spontaneity was her middle name, and one of my favorite things about her was that she would just kind of drop in from time to time and do life with me – adjusting to whatever was already on my schedule. We had journeyed closely alongside each other for a few years now, as we had been living in the same city. She had even been my neighbor during the first year. We could share the important things in life with each other, and even though we were very different, we shared an important devotion to living out God's will for our lives. Our friendship came with interruptions, though, as her spontaneity led her on many different travels - often back to her childhood home in Africa.
Lately, I had been a little bit annoyed with her sudden disappearances, and I wanted to blame it on her having commitment issues and so on, but after a moment of introspection, I found out that it had nothing to do with her and everything to do with me. She was a free bird, whom I wanted to keep in a cage, because I loved her and wanted her around, even though I knew it was wrong. Truth be told, I was a little jealous of her life of adventures, when I compared it to my own life grounded in commitments and routines. A part of me wanted to just fly out with her.

Though being apart for long periods of time, there was never a doubt that she was always there for me, and I would always be there for her. We learned to set each other free to follow the paths God was leading us on individually, and when our paths crossed again, we caught up on lost times and were blessed by hearing about and sharing all that God was doing in each of our lives.

A FAMILY WEDDING
July 2021

My little sister's wedding was one of those weddings where I knew most of the guests, so it was an amazing day filled with good talks and interactions. The weather was nice, my sister was beautiful and happy, and it brought me joy to see all the love and appreciation she received from all their wedding guests. In his speech, her husband mentioned that he was very happy to be the one with whom she would share the deepest things in life, and I felt a sweet longing for one day getting to experience that same level of intimacy with another person.

It was perhaps a little bit unusual that both of us older sisters were still single, while our baby sister as only a 21-year-old was ready to step into marriage so far ahead of us. To me, though, it wasn't much of a problem. This past year had been an amazing year of freedom from being interested in anyone. God had been allowed to do His work in expanding my perspective on life, and it had been one of the best years of my life so far. Now I would be embarking on a whole new adventure with Him, and this had taken up far more space in my mind lately than the deceitful, ancient voice that asked me if a blessing hadn't passed me and my older sister by, as we watched our younger sister walk down the aisle. Some voices are not worth listening to, and I had told God that I didn't mind waiting. I wanted more out of a marriage anyway than what my current circle of friends could offer. I trusted God that the new path in front of me would open doors and expand my network, and that He would not fail in providing me with a spouse down the road, who would want to join me on the crazy faith adventure that I hoped my life would someday become.

Towards the end of the party, I talked to the parents of my new brother-in-law, and they reminded me that everything good comes to those who wait. They emphasized the importance of finding a man of real quality. *"And they are out there"* his dad added, to which his mom suggested that *"there might even have been a few of them at the party today."* My sister and her husband did indeed have friends of the highest quality, and especially one of them had unexpectedly left me with a very good impression. I had known about him for years, but this day I got to see for myself his wisdom, his heart for serving others, and a lot of other good qualities.

Earlier that night, we had found out that we were both going to do the church leadership program. As we were talking, I felt excited about all the new adventures to come and for the first time in a long time, I found myself standing in front of a guy that I genuinely wanted to get to know better.

FIRST-DAY FEELINGS
August 2021

In August, I packed my car and drove to the school that hosted the introduction week of the church leadership program. A few weeks prior, I had been added to a Facebook group with the other people, who were going to join the program, and to my surprise, one of my old boarding school friends would be part of the team as well. The two of us were different as night and day, but an unlikely friendship had formed between us, as we had engaged in various projects together. After boarding school, our connection had turned into one of those friendships where you lose contact, but reconnect well every time you run into each other, and a few years ago, I got to hear her beautiful story of coming back to Jesus after having been away from Him for a longer period of time. My heart rejoiced that our paths now crossed again, and that we would get to journey side by side for a season in this program.

I did not expect the slap of inferiority that hit me when I arrived at the school. I never struggled much with feeling less than others in my life, although I was familiar with the feeling of being overlooked in the crowd. I always enjoyed close friendships with a few people, who got the opportunity to see and know the depths of me. On the larger arenas of life, however, I was shy and usually preferred to keep myself in the background, and when you don't draw attention to yourself, you often remain anonymous.

Now, when I compared myself to the other people in the group, I questioned what I was even doing there in the company of people with much stronger personalities and seemingly more confident plans for their futures in ministry. I didn't even know if I wanted to be a pastor. The only thing I knew for certain was that God for some reason wanted me to do this program now. My doubts only grew, when one of the teachers came by and unwisely made a comment on how he hadn't seen it coming that I would want to be a pastor. I didn't think he even knew me well enough to make a statement like that so right at that moment, I was completely ready to just go home again.

A while later, I was sitting outside, talking to two of the other girls in the program. One of them told me that as we had made our round of introductions earlier, she had felt so strongly that I was in the right place, and that God truly wanted me there in the group. This was some much-needed confirmation. I still didn't know where God wanted me to end up with this program, but I was ready to take it all in and find out as He would hopefully reveal more along the way.

WORK IN PROGRESS
September 2021

At the end of summer, I was hit by the reality of all the responsibilities I had taken on in this new season. As a part of the church leadership program, it was the plan for me to try out different areas of ministry in my local church, so I would be able to become a good leader or pastor one day. My pastor was great at letting me step in and explore opportunities wherever I felt like it, but even though almost all options were open, I struggled with finding an area that felt just right. What came closest was maybe when I got the opportunity to prepare teachings and for that reason, I had happily accepted the invitation to preach on the first evening of our annual church camp.

The church camp took place at the end of the first week of September, and this same week marked the start of my master's studies. This meant that I had two incredibly packed days of information and teambuilding activities prior to the camp, and I had to go directly from the festivities there to the location of the camp a few hours' drive away. The evening before, I had gotten a rejection on an application regarding financial aid for my commute to the university, while my friend's application had gone through. It felt unfair, and sudden worries about my financial situation had been rumbling around in my mind to such a degree that I had gotten almost no sleep that night.

On my way to the camp, I got stuck in a traffic jam on the highway, and I knew it would severely delay my arrival, which was not great, when I was the preacher for the night. While sitting in the car, a cold that had been on its way all week suddenly flared up, making my head feel like it was about to explode. When I finally arrived at the camp, I had a massive breakdown and couldn't seem to stop crying again. I felt fragile and in no condition to stand up in front of our entire church and share the word of God with confidence and conviction. My youth pastor's wife stepped in to encourage me and help me gather my thoughts. When I told her about the rejected application, she calmly suggested that maybe God wanted to work with my need for control in this area of my life. That through this experience, He would maybe teach me to trust Him more with my finances. And she was right. Money had never been in short supply in my life so far, and now I was drowning in worries about the prospect of losing only some of it.

As I finally stood on stage that night, preaching, I shared a message very close to my heart about letting go of dreams in our lives in exchange for God's "more", and many people had an encounter with God, even though I felt incredibly vulnerable and cried my way through it. It felt odd to me how I could be so worried about my finances in one moment and in the next, I could testify about God's faithfulness in my life.
Maybe it was because I was on the way. God works in areas at the time, and even though several areas were under construction right now, there was also a work that He had already done. It felt good to know that He was willing to use me already where I was in my journey now – even with all my raw edges and unfinished processes, and even though there was still so much more to become in the future.

PARKING LOT EPIPHANY

September 2021

Almost every day, I commuted to a larger city an hour's drive away for my studies, and I quickly found out, what times I could easily find parking around the university, and what times I should just park further away and walk down to the faculty buildings. One Monday morning, on a typical "find parking elsewhere" time, I chose to drive down the parking lot at the school and check for parking, anyway. After all, I only needed one empty space. I passed row after row of occupied spaces, and slowly lost hope of finding one. *"I should have just parked somewhere else,"* I told myself. But then, in the very last row closest to the building, where my class would take place, there was exactly one empty space. I parked, while rejoicing and thanking God for saving me the very best space on the entire parking lot. As I turned off the engine, I strongly felt God speaking to me, telling me to stay in the car, as He wanted to tell me something based on the experience, I just had.

He gently showed me that just as I could think it was impossible to find an empty parking spot in the business faculty parking lot, in the same way, it could sometimes feel impossible for me to find those destinations in life that I was searching for. I could have that feeling of passing one after another and for different reasons, they were just not for me. Eventually, my hope of ever finding it would maybe even slowly start to die out. But then He encouraged me with the promise that He had a place "reserved" for me, just like He had reserved this parking spot for me. I got the feeling that through this experience, God told me that I would have to wait longer yet for it to happen in my life, but I also felt reassured that I wouldn't wait in vain.

There is an element of faith in having to wait for something. Sometimes, when doors close or no doors seem to open for the things we deeply long for, it can be God's loving invitation for us to go further and deeper with Him, until we reach a place where we are ready to receive what's best for us. God knew that I would have gladly taken any empty spot I might have found on my way down the parking lot, and thus, lost the opportunity of the very best one closest to the building. Waiting well will sometimes mean for us to move past what could be good things, trusting that He, who is faithful and loves us the most, has the very best reserved for us, if we will only hand Him our timelines.

SIGNIFICANT
October 2021

On a random evening in October, while I was unlocking the front door to my apartment after a long day of studies, I heard in my mind the words "*You're significant!*" A few seconds went by, before it occurred to me that these words in no way fit into the line of thoughts, I had going on in that moment, and that it was probably the Holy Spirit talking to me. I loved the contrast of God speaking those words to me on such a random weekday evening, while I was doing something as ordinary as opening my front door.

I didn't throw around the word "significant" a lot in my everyday sentences, so I placed myself on the couch and looked it up in a dictionary. This is how I found out that God had just told me that He found me *important enough to be worthy of attention*. To me - someone who often felt like a wallflower - this was a huge substantial declaration of love from God, and more so, it spoke into the calling He had put on my life.

I found it challenging, on the one hand to have a sense of a great calling on my life, and on the other hand to accept the ordinariness of my upbringing, my current life circumstances, and my life choices. In many ways, I felt very anonymous, and I had a hard time seeing how God would move me from where I was now and into that destiny that He had begun speaking to me about. I couldn't even express with words what it would be going to look like. Maybe my spirit knew something that the rest of me still couldn't quite fathom. And maybe I wasn't supposed to know yet. After all, Jesus called Simon Peter a rock long before he had developed any rock-like qualities in his life, so when He told me that I was significant, there would probably be a journey ahead of me, before I would fully grow into the fullness of that word.

A SNOWSTORM STORY
December 2021

I found an amazing new group of friends within the church leadership program, whom I could relate to and have fun with every sixth week, when we met up for a week of theology studies. During one of those weeks in December, we planned to go to a nearby city for dinner, and even though a snowstorm had been raging for hours, we decided to drive out in a minibus, anyways. As unwise as it would have been for us to just drive out, yet another level of stupidity would quickly add to the first one. We realized the magnitude of the snowstorm by the line of cars on the main road and the tilted bus in the ditch that met us when we got out of town, but instead of going back, someone suggested taking the small roads instead, and for some reason that was what we ended up doing.

We didn't drive for long, before we met an oncoming car that was stuck on the road. We couldn't get around it without driving too far out into the dangerous snow-filled side of the road, - a move that would certainly result in our car getting stuck too, so the only other solution was for all of us to go out and help free the other car. It was completely impossible to see anything, as snow whipped against our faces the moment we stepped outside. But somehow, we managed to free the car and continued our trip, arriving safely at the restaurant an hour and a half later.

After a peaceful meal, we went back out in the storm, and this time it would only get more dramatic. Twice we got stuck, waiting in a line of cars, and the second time we were there for almost half an hour, before we sent one of our friends out to see, why we were even in that line in the first place. We quickly lost sight of him, panicked, and began driving past the other cars to at least pick him up again. We then found out that there was no reason for the line at all and drove on, until we were suddenly stuck and thought "*that's it - we are now going to spend the night here with no food, no toilet, no anything.*" That was until our appointed chauffeur managed to do something, and the car slowly started moving again. We all laughed and screamed in relief, completely high on the adrenaline rush of it all. Like in an apocalypse, we drove past car after car that had been abandoned on the side of the road, while we congratulated ourselves on surviving our own stupidity. We talked about how this was the kind of story that you might hear the preacher tell in a sermon, and after returning home safely, I reflected a little bit more on the experience we had just had. This was indeed a story worth telling. A story full of adventure, drama, intense feelings, great people, and most importantly - a faithful God that would come through and write a happy ending, and I felt lucky to have one of those stories to tell – one that would hopefully be just one out of many more to come.

NO ONE'S PUPPET

March 2022

At a national leadership conference in March, my pastor and I had been invited on stage for an interview on the topic of fostering new leaders. Here, I shared a little bit of my journey, from God's invitation for me to join the church leadership program, to the people who impacted me along the way, and the love for church that had grown bigger in my heart during the last few years.

Before the interview, the interviewer and I had been shortly introduced, and here I got a nagging feeling that I might have been singled out among my peers in the program, because I was a female. I cringed at the thought that I might have been put on stage just to prove a point that there was still some work to be done towards having more female pastors in the network. My fears were confirmed, when I was asked the question of whether I saw any challenges or obstacles down the road of this journey. I was in no way confident that I represented the upcoming female pastor, for whom they wanted to make better conditions in the network, and I hated the thought of being put in a box like that. I didn't even know if I wanted to become a pastor, but all around I saw faces that seemed to expect this ministry to be my destination.

Truth be told, I did have some reservations about stepping into church leadership. The prospect of leading a church seemed incredibly lonely to me. And maybe these thoughts didn't belong in the 21st century, but I especially didn't want to be a leader if my husband was not going to be. I would prefer to not be a front-runner. It seemed like my temperament and nature better allowed me to take on a supporting role, which was what I dreamt of doing. What I was trying to figure out, though, was whether these reservations were natural reactions to me trying to fit myself into a mold in which I didn't belong, or whether they were fear-based excuses for not going where God would want me to go. If the latter, I knew these excuses would have to be overcome, just like Moses had to overcome his speech problems, Gideon had to overcome his low self-esteem, and Jeremiah had to overcome his age, when God called them to do a great task.

But that was the whole thing - God had never spoken to me about becoming a pastor. He only asked me to follow Him into the program, and I could easily find several other reasons for Him to do that. That's why it hurt so much when I tried to process some of these reservations with people I respected and looked up to, and they all just assumed that they were excuses for me to overcome. I always ended up feeling misunderstood. I knew I had to walk this journey closely with God and become everything He would want me to become, but it was important to me to be able to own my own journey and my own destination without being conformed to any expectations that other people or a church network in need of female pastors, might put on me.

FOOLISH HOPES
April 2022

I was chatting with a good friend of mine, and when our conversation casually turned to the topic of romance, I told her a little bit about my interest in this guy in the program. She knew him as well and with a regretful expression, she let me know that he was already seeing someone. My reaction to this information embarrassed me, to say the least. A deep feeling of disappointment hit me, and I couldn't stop the tears from welling up in my eyes. I was very aware that it was an overreaction of dimensions - I didn't know this guy enough to even call him my friend, but somehow, I had built a hope around him in my mind that came tumbling down with a force, I didn't realize I had allowed it to gain.

What actually happened, was that I had put my hope and trust in something I could see rather than mainly trusting God's character and love for me. It was clear to me that this guy was limited edition, and I didn't see anyone else out there, who came even close to matching his character and devotion to God. Now that he was unavailable, it made me feel almost like God had failed in taking my dreams into account, as I couldn't see other prospects of someone, who could join me in the life and ministry, I was heading towards. In that moment, I saw clearly, exactly how small my trust in God was in this area of my life, and I had to repent my unbelief.

I found out later that the guy wasn't in fact seeing anyone, but the experience had given me a much-needed wakeup call to not let my mind run away with me. I wanted to trust God's timing and the work He was doing in my life in this season.

A FRIENDSHIP FROM GOD
July 2022

I was lonely. The emotion had crept into my life so slowly that I didn't even realize it, until I found myself walking around like a balloon that would burst any minute, because I had kept so much to myself for so long, with no one to share it with. My two best friends had been traveling all spring, other good friends had slowly moved away for studies in bigger cities, some were now occupied with relationships, and some friendships were just not the same anymore, because we had grown apart. I had been so busy with work, church, and studies all year that I had hardly noticed it, but now I looked around and thought *"who do I actually have in my life to talk to right now?"*

During my summer break, I went to a youth camp and here, I randomly bonded with a cool girl over our shared love for soda and checklists. One afternoon, when the program allowed for a break, we sat down in a couple of soft chairs with each our soda, and we had the best talk I had had for a very long time. With tears in our eyes, we shared our mutual experience of having a calling on our lives to the church, the feeling of loneliness accompanied with serving in a small-town church, the feeling of losing friendships in our twenties, the dream of serving together with a husband, the fear of having to do ministry alone, the attacks we experienced on being single, and the feeling that God in this season was calling us to Himself. Our tears turned to laughter as we thanked God for this new friendship that He had so clearly gifted us with. Everything that had completely consumed me and weighed me down for so long, now felt like an easier burden to carry, because I felt seen and understood by my new friend. God had given me someone with whom I could once again share the deepest things of my heart, - someone who fit into this season of my journey. She was an answer to a prayer I hadn't even prayed, but it was a testimony of a God, who loved me very much. Sometimes, we may have to wait long to see His promises fulfilled in our lives, but He is faithful to provide us with what we need on our journey to get there.

GET OUT OF THE TOWER!
July 2022

Apparently, God speaks through Disney movies. A girl at the youth camp got a word for me from the movie Tangled. She got the feeling that I related to the song "*When will my life begin?*", sung by the main character in the beginning of the movie, as she daydreams about escaping from the tower. Now, the girl at youth camp believed that God was telling me to get out of my very own version of that tower.

The word really hit home for me, and a few weeks later, a woman from my church gave me a similar word. Further, I had recently been drawn to movies about main characters, who ditched other people's expectations, took a risk, and broke out of the daily grind to go on an adventure that would cause them to find deeper happiness elsewhere.

I longed for adventures that my current situation in life didn't allow me to live out. I believed this was God inviting me to take charge of my own life, let go of other people's expectations of me, and follow Him into the unknown for greater adventures. I had no idea what it would look like, but I desperately wanted to escape the tower of responsibilities and obligations that made up my entire life right now.

GARDEN BADMINTON
July 2022

We had enjoyed some great days at my parents' place. I treasured these times where we would all meet up again and spend time together playing games, making waffles, and having barbecues or bonfires every evening.

This particular evening, my sisters brought back an old family tradition – garden badminton. I couldn't count the number of hours we had spent playing badminton on our family vacations during our childhood and teenage years. On all quiet summer evenings, when the wind subsided, we would set up the net on the lawn by the summer house and go play. It was one of my favorite family bonding activities, as it always filled the air with fun and laughter. The same was true this evening. They all teamed up two and two and got something of a tournament going on. Meanwhile, I was sitting on the patio, reading a book and as time went by, a slow sadness crept over me. I wanted to join in on the fun, but I was reluctant to, because I was aware that in doing so, I would break up their teams. There used to be no set teams in our family, - we would mix it up all the time. Now both of my sisters, as well as my parents, had somewhat of a more fixed teammate, and although I knew how irrational it was, I suddenly felt left out of more than just a beloved family tradition.

My family was changing. Nothing would ever be the same, and as both of my sisters had now found the person they wanted to create new traditions with, I felt like the only one in my family, who still wished that we could sometimes go back to how things used to be, when it was just the five of us. Our dynamics were changing, and I missed what I used to share with my sisters. I suddenly struggled to find my place within my own family. I knew it was very normal and natural for families to change like this, when you and your siblings were all grown up, but I guess I just wished that I wouldn't somehow feel so left behind in the process.

INSTAGRAM INTEGRITY
August 2022

I felt convicted, as I listened to a sermon in which the pastor emphasized that being a Christian will most likely cost you something, socially. As far as I recalled, I never experienced anyone pulling away from me, due to my association with Jesus. But that was probably the thing: I rarely spoke about Him. This was something I wanted to change, so I went home and made an Instagram post with a picture of my church where I invited everyone who wanted to, to come and join me for a service. I was terrified, and I hesitated for a long time before hitting "post", and that was where I realized, how much my fear of man still held me back. Afterwards, though, I felt good about having taken the stance that I just did.

A few weeks went by, and then one day, I got a message from a girl, who used to be part of the youth group in the church where I grew up. She had been away from church for some years, and now she found herself missing it, so when she saw my post on Instagram, she just knew that she had to write to me. We met up, and I got to bring her to our youth group. I was beyond thrilled to discover that my post had been for someone, and it made me reflect: *I wonder how much more people we would get to lead to Christ, if we just dared to open our mouths and speak more openly about our faith?* At least I knew that I wanted a life full of these testimonies of people who discovered or rediscovered Jesus, because they saw or heard of Him through me.

SYMPTOMS OF BURNOUT
September 2022

As school started, I found myself having frequent outbursts of violent crying. I knew I was not doing well, but it scared me how it had suddenly come so far that my body no longer allowed me to keep it in.

I went to talk to my pastor, and he gave me the advice to fill up my calendar with more energy inducers to balance out the number of energy drainers in my life. After another breakdown on a Sunday morning in church, one of my friends gave me similar advice of going away for some time with a couple of good friends. I genuinely thought it was good advice, but I couldn't even muster the energy to make the changes.

Every day, when I was done with all that was required of me, I let myself fall on to the couch and stayed there, until I had somewhere to be again. Even small tasks had begun to seem unmanageably, and I procrastinated with everything. I didn't eat healthy. My dishes were standing around for days, before I managed to clean them. I watched way too much TV, and I spent way too much time alone. And then I managed to beat myself up about it as well. I felt ashamed, somehow. *"Of course, I am not doing better, when I am allowing all these bad habits in my life,"* I would tell myself. I knew very well that I was the only source of change for my situation, but I was too busy running around, meeting other people's expectations and needs that there was absolutely no more energy for me to spend on my own physical and mental health. So I just stumbled forward one day at a time.

When was the last time, I had laughed? I couldn't remember. I never really laughed anymore. Joy was gone. I knew it had been there earlier in my life, but it felt as in another lifetime that I had lived a life in bright colors. Now everything around me just seemed gloomy and grey.

I felt so incredibly stuck. I looked back to happier times and realized that I would never have those times back. The time of my friendship group from boarding school was over, and the same was true for my friendship group from church. It would never be the same again, as we all lived in different places, grew apart, found ourselves in different life stages, and so on. And it was not that I wanted to have that time back, but I dwelt with the memories, because these were friendships that once brought me happiness, and I desperately tried to find out, what I could do to get back my joy. The doors to the past, however, were all closed. Even if I tried to bring some of it back into my life, I wasn't sure that it would make me happy anymore.

Then I looked ahead, and there were no secure prospects in any area of my life. No specific job after graduation next summer, no specific ministry, no place to live, no spouse. I desperately wanted certainty in just one area of my future, but no doors were open here either.

DREAMS OF A STUDY BUDDY

October 2022

At a family birthday in October, I was talking to my grandma, and as I updated her on my church leadership program, she shared this dream with me that she had recently had. She told me how she had seen me there, sitting in a classroom with the others, deeply immersed in my studies, and that she had seen a young man there, also immersed in his studies until one day, he had asked me, if I wouldn't just want to come study at his place. I kept that dream close to my heart, because somehow, it resonated deeply with something I was hoping and longing for. I hoped that the guy that I would someday marry, would have a calling to ministry, but more than that, I hoped that we would be able to share a love for theology, knowledge, literature, art, poetry, wisdom, and all the deeper things in life that had always been such a treasured thing to me.

Growing up, my favorite books were the ones about Anne of Green Gables, and I was particularly in awe of the relationship between Anne and Gilbert. I used to joke around with the fact that he, a fictional character, set the standard for my future husband, and it wasn't completely untrue. His character was one thing, but I longed for that friendship that the author so beautifully portrayed in her books. In the contexts of the real world though, this didn't seem attainable to me. It appeared to me that when I met guys with potential, I always became hyper self-aware and thus, had no prerequisites of getting to know them well. On the other hand, the friendships I did manage to build, were never ones with romantic potential. I struggled to see how I would ever find both in one person. But then again, it would only take one, and I wanted to trust that God was good enough to help me find what had been my biggest dream, since I was a little girl.

TIDES OF CHANGE
November 2022

November came around, and in my heart, I felt that big changes were just around the corner for me. I was excited about it, because the last year had left me more exhausted than I cared to admit.

In the beginning of the month, my older sister broke the news on her engagement, and my heart cried out in joy for her. She deserved this happiness after some very tough years, and I knew she had found one of the good ones. For me too, a hope that had been in my heart for a long time now finally seemed to materialize itself in something tangible, and I was equally excited and scared. "*Stuff like this doesn't happen to me,*" I kept repeating to myself. It seemed too good to be true, but I guessed that was the beauty of grace. I was overwhelmed with the fact that God in His goodness was finally answering such a specific prayer of mine. It filled my heart with joy that my phone would now often light up with a name that for so long had been just the name of some ideal stranger, but now became increasingly familiar to me as we exchanged messages and got to know each other better. Nothing had been said to define the relationship, but even though I was scared to deceive myself, I knew that I would have to take this leap of faith for my love story, because this guy seemed far worth the risk.

Around the same time, I got the first notions that there would potentially be an open position for me in church after my graduation this summer, and I suddenly began to feel God's provision in several areas of my future where I had earlier only felt uncertainty. I received a prophetic word from someone that my next couple of years would be filled with huge changes in several areas of my life, but that God wanted to let me know that He had a plan with all of it, and that I shouldn't be afraid. I was excited. I had prayed for new adventures and yet felt stuck for so long, but now finally, it seemed that God would lead me into a new season with all the change I had been longing for. I deeply wanted to follow His lead into the transformation of my entire life and to not fear the process ahead.

TOO GOOD TO BE TRUE

January 2023

I went on my official first date in the beginning of January, and I was so nervous that I could've passed out. Exchanging messages was one thing, but as I entered the bus station and saw him standing there in person, it suddenly felt like there was a weird gap of connecting the guy I had been writing with for the past few months to this guy standing in front of me in flesh and blood. Though I felt awkward and nervous the entire time, the hours we spent together were not at all bad for a first date. He was a perfect gentleman, paid for my food, held the door for me, and carried my bag as we walked around the city in the early evening. The way he looked at me and smiled, and the way he gently put his hand on my back when we crossed a road, all filled my already nervous stomach with severe amounts of butterflies.

We shared a moment at a place with a great view over all the city lights, and later as we said goodbye at the bus station, he made sure to tell me that he would like for us to meet up again. What kept going around in my head for the rest of the night was how on earth I had been so lucky as to win the interest of this guy. It all seemed too good to be true.

THE IMPORTANCE OF PACE
March 2023

As exciting as the new year had started off, the first two months turned out to be overwhelming, to say the least. The final semester of my studies meant thesis writing, and what was supposed to be a precious time of immersing myself into a topic of my own choosing, looked more like the last mandatory sprint, before I could allow myself to completely collapse on the other side of the finish line.
I had decided to scale up my responsibility in our youth group as well, because I felt that it would be the right thing for me to do, but I felt horribly alone in the role of leadership. My refuge place in all of it was spending time with my new friend, and we commuted back and forth between our cities, making lots of time in our busy schedules to invest into this new relationship. However, I would soon have my place of escape invaded by fears and worries.

At the end of January, I made it clear to my leaders that I would be happy to spend another year fully investing in our church. I dreamt of doing ministry, and I didn't know what else I would want to do with my next year, so it seemed to me like the right next step to take.
A few days later, when I shared it with my friend, he initially encouraged me, but later as I was on my way home, he asked me when I would know about it for sure, because that decision might potentially have implications for the future of our relationship. I froze as it dawned upon me what he meant. Of course he was allowed to think so, but it completely caught me by surprise. To me, the geographic distance between us would never be a dealbreaker, and it made me feel very disposable that it might be for him. He could tell that I was upset, but I was not able to communicate properly in that moment. Honestly, I was too scared to say anything that would cause him to call it quits right away. How could I explain to him that I was knocked out for a moment by the realization that I was not nearly as important to him as he was to me?

We decided to give our relationship more time, even though the threat of "after summer" now hang above it like a stormy cloud. It suddenly felt like

I was being put on trial. How much time would he be willing to give us? It felt like I had to make an effort to prove myself good enough for him, but I didn't know how to be anything but myself, and I had a horrible feeling that it maybe wasn't going to be enough for him. It all made me very anxious, but I knew what I wanted, so I kept going, hoping that we would be able to find a common pace in time.

That wasn't what happened, though. Within a few months, I could feel him slowly pulling away and making less of an effort, and at the end of March, when he told me that we needed to have a talk after a horrible week of doubt and uncertainty, I knew exactly what was coming for me.
He let me down very gently. He made sure to let me know that whoever ended up with me, would be a lucky man. I don't know why guys in general think this is a comforting thing to tell a girl in the moment of a breakup. It might be true, but it felt very much like he just wanted to rub me off of himself by using his words to throw me in the direction of someone else, and that was just hurtful, when I hadn't even been given time to mourn what I had just lost.
I wanted to ask him to give us more time, but I knew it wouldn't make a difference. His mind was clearly made up. When he left, I felt a sense of peace, because now at least I had clarity after weeks of hardcore anxiety.

The next day, when I went to talk to my mentor, she made me aware that even though this guy was a good one, who was running in a good direction, he was maybe running too fast for me. He hadn't been able to slow down long enough to really see the gold in me, and I deserved to not have to chase after someone, but to know that I was enough by just being me. It would take some time for me to realize the truth in those words. Sometimes two people just don't move through life at the same pace, and you shouldn't try to keep up with them at the cost of letting yourself down.

AN EASTER ANALOGY
April 2023

*D*ear God,
I find it extremely difficult to be home at my parents' place during this Easter break. I am facing my disappointment again and again. I reminisce about Christmas time and all the hope I had for a budding relationship as we exchanged messages every day. A light had been lit, and there was hope even though it was in its beginning stages. And now I'm standing here, and I am forced to bury the hope I once had. I think about the disciples. How they experienced Easter and the defeat when Jesus had been killed on the cross.

They probably thought they had his plan figured out, but they had to endure disappointment, pain, sorrow, and discouragement as they were forced to bury everything they had thought would come to past and see Him lie there in the grave. I feel the disappointment and the discouragement here in my Easter, while I attempt to bury and mourn and make sense of these past few months. The disciples didn't understand. I don't understand.

But Sunday is coming. Jesus was not buried to stay in the grave but to be resurrected and to save all of humanity. The sorrow was turned into joy. The disciples had to endure the disappointment and the hurt without understanding what He was doing, but they were about to see how it would all lead to something far greater than what they imagined. And that gives me hope here on my Friday where I experience the disappointment of everything that didn't become what I hoped for, and where I am forced to bury what I invested my heart, my dreams, and my hope into. I feel all the discouragement and the pain of what I have lost.

But I know there will be a Sunday. I know that what I buried in tears will lead to a resurrection in joy. That there are bigger things out there for me than what I lost. That there is no pain and sorrow without a greater course, which will be good.

I know my Sunday is coming.

WIDE-OPEN SPACES
April 2023

The experience of the last few months hurt far more than I would ever admit to him. We had built our dating relationship from the ground, but with the expansive amount of time and emotions I had invested into it, coupled with all the intensity of "firsts" it brought along for me, it had caused me to build up a tower where he had built only a half wall. It hurts far less to jump back to ground zero from a half wall than it does jumping from the top of a tower. After he called it quits, and all interaction between us ceased to what it had been before (none), I simply couldn't understand how an action that left me in pieces could simultaneously allow him to walk away without any bruises, whatsoever. How could something that had been so valuable to me be so easy for him to just abandon?

He'd told me he needed someone that he could laugh and have fun with. Nothing about my life felt like that right now. The heartbreak of this loss made the fragile structures that made up the rest of my life bend over and crash. For a little while, the relationship had sparked some new energy into my life, but now the exhaustion that had been building up for so long came back in full scale and knocked me to the ground. I completely abandoned my intentions of taking over the role as youth leader, and I dropped all my current responsibilities to the floor. My love for people was gone, and it felt like all the people in my life only wanted something from me. I had nothing left to give, and I wanted everyone to leave me alone.
My capacity only allowed for me to write on my thesis, and as soon as my writing buddy left for the day, I collapsed on the couch, sopping and distracting myself from the heartache with series and movies. But there was no real escaping it. I had so much pain on the inside that it spilled out and I spent hours crying every night, building big piles of Kleenex tissues on the floor next to my bed.

I began to dream about escaping again. It felt like my city was closing in on me, but I didn't know if it was really God, who let me know that my time here had come to an end, or if I should stay and trust God to provide for me, relationally. I hated the thought of disappointing the people in my church, and when they wanted to invest in me and give me a great opportunity for ministry, wouldn't I be a fool to just turn my back on that? On the other hand, my future in the church leadership program was now muddied with the pain of having to do it alongside the guy, who had just broken my heart, and I found myself confused about my future in that area as well.

Truth be told, I was disappointed with God. I had believed that this relationship was a long-awaited, grace-filled gift from Him, and I didn't understand, why He would take it away from me again. I thought I had found a guy that understood the kind of life that I wanted to live with God, and who would be an amazing fit for me in the life of faith adventures and ministry that made up my envisioned future. And I couldn't see anyone else out there that would measure up even the smallest bit.

In many ways my future was now a blank canvas where everything was possible, but I didn't have the strength to seize the opportunities. I looked around, and I saw no one who would join me on the adventures I longed for in my life. There is this deep sense of loneliness accompanied with walking through a valley of shadows. No one, not even your closest friends or family can take the pain away from you and heal your heart. I felt isolated and alone, and I had a terrifying fear that I would stay that way and end up that way.

The wide-open space in front of me felt threatening. As far as I could see, there were just open waters of uncertainty, and I desperately looked for small pieces of land out there in the horizon, testifying to me that everything would be okay again. But nothing was in sight. I had passed the isle of a relationship that I had spent years hoping for, and now there were no prospects of a suitable life partner in sight. I would soon pass the isle of graduation, leaving the safety of the educational system behind and be forced to figure out how to provide an income for myself. I would soon pass the isle of moving out of my home as my apartment was tied to the fact that I was a university student, and then I would have to find another home. I wanted to leave the isle of my current city behind, but where would I move to? Every area of my life was shaking underneath me, and I was dead scared, and dead burned out. I knew my only solution would be to cling to Jesus with everything I had left in me, and trust that He would lead me over these scary open waters, so that's what I did. Every day, I poured out my heart and pain to him, reminding Him again and again about His promises to me (as if He would forget), and somewhere in the deepest place of my heart, I knew that He was right there with me, and that this complete loss of control was strengthening my faith. He wouldn't fail in using it for something good that I had yet to see.

25
May 2023

For my 25th birthday, I invited a bunch of my friends by for a picnic in the park right next to my apartment complex. The idea of filling the day with some kind of activity was more attractive to me than sitting at home alone, wallowing in my pain. Truth be told, though, I really just wanted to get past this day. In Denmark, we have this tradition that if you are unmarried at the age of 25, you get showered in cinnamon as a dear reminder of the fact that you are not yet married at this age. Traditionally, I think it was directed towards men, who didn't want to step up and commit to a woman, but as it often happens with traditions, they slowly cross the boundaries of their original context and content. From the bottom of my heart, I hated this tradition, and even more so as I approached my 25th birthday, not only unmarried, but also very heartbroken. It was simply beyond me, how people could be so insensitive as to know what I was going through and still care more about upholding a silly tradition, which I believed more often than not was just salt in the wounds of people, who had to wait longer than many others to find their person to marry.

My 25th birthday also allowed me to open a letter that 14-year-old Line had written to her future self. I was a little afraid of the feelings that reading this letter might evoke in me. Would I be a disappointment to her? Had I let her down?

The letter turned out to be harmless, except from one thing that stuck with me. 14-year-old Line had big, creative dreams for her life, and she wanted to let future Line know, that she would be very disappointed, if she had turned out to become just another ordinary office mouse. One part of me laughed a little bit about younger Line's big aspirations that hadn't yet been tested and molded by real life. However, another part of me felt convicted as my educational choices would lead me straight in the direction that was such an awful prospect to teenage Line. I still longed for something more in life than a nine-to-five job. I wanted to make a real impact. I wanted to take risks and create beautiful things. I wanted to learn something from the pure heart of 14-year-old Line, who hadn't yet con-formed herself to mediocrity, and I wanted to make her proud.

GROWING INTO A CHILD
May 2023

I knew I had carried way too much responsibility for way too long. Everywhere I looked in my life, I just saw expectations. I saw my dad's expectations for me to finish my master's degree. I saw my pastors' expectations for me to take my responsibility for the youth group seriously in this season. I saw the expectations of the youth that something would be planned out for them in our youth ministry. I saw the expectations of our church network that I would become a pastor to meet their need for female pastors. I saw my thesis partner's expectations for me to spend all my time on our thesis. I felt the expectations of the business faculty that I would make a grand career for myself. I saw my own expectations for myself to meet everyone's expectations, and in shame, I had to admit that I also sometimes thought these were all God's expectations for me, and that He would only be satisfied with me when I had met all of them.

One night, I wrote the following in my journal:

I just want to laugh and have fun. But I have been a grown-up for so long that I forgot how to do that. I am honestly afraid that it is too late for me to be young. That I used my chance, and now the doors of opportunities are closed. Most of my friends move towards marriage and kids now, or they work full-time jobs and have studies. I am afraid there is no longer any room for spontaneity, slumber parties, hiking trips, or birthday parties like there was a few years ago. It makes me feel lonely and abandoned.

At the age of 25, I fell into the belief that my youth was officially over, and there would be no chance for me to experience what belonged to happier times in the past. That there would be no chance of regaining my joy, which had been stolen from me. That there would be no chance to escape the isolation and loneliness I had fallen into. I had no idea how to change the trajectory of my life, but I desperately wanted God to teach me how to be a child again and give me back my freedom, laughter, and joy.

TRANSPLANTING TIME
June 2023

When I had conquered the mountain of handing in my thesis, and I had nothing left to do but wait for my final exam, I could no longer postpone the question of what was going to happen after summer. Different ideas had already been rumbling in the back of my mind for months, but none of them seemed ideal. Then one day, God reminded me of an image from one of my old biology books. It was an image of a wooden barrel, and the barrel was a visual representation of a law called the law of the minimum. The law of the minimum expresses the principle that plant growth is limited by the resource that is least available at the growth site. In the image from my biology book, the different resources were represented by a wooden plank each, and the length of the planks represented the available amount of that resource. Thus, water would run out of the barrel at the point of the shortest plank, even though the barrel had potential to contain more water. This made me ponder the question of what was the least available resource in my life at the moment? In what area of my life was I bleeding to such a degree that it hindered my overall thriving and flourishing?

I knew it. I was in desperate need of like-minded friends, with whom I could have fun and share my everyday life. This was the main factor I would have to place myself after, and that was when Bible college resurfaced in my mind. It had already crossed my mind a few times during the spring, but I had dismissed it, regarding it a setback to go there when the whole world was open to me. That was just the thing, though. For so long, I had been trying to do everything at once and embrace all the opportunities that presented themselves to me, but I could no longer keep that pace. Burned out and defeated, I was reminded of the fact that I was human, and that I had very human needs that I had neglected for too long.

I surrendered my pride and signed up for the school, telling God that this would be my plan after summer, unless He told me otherwise (and He was <u>very</u> welcome to do so). Then I dragged myself across the finish line of my studies, having earned a degree that had killed me to an extent that I didn't at all feel like celebrating it. I looked around at my fellow graduates and felt a sense of jealousy about the fact that they could now go out and show off their degree to the world, while mine would just be put on a shelf to collect dust in this next season.

Sometimes, however, we must be brave and choose to do something completely different than what is expected of us. I wanted to be brave enough to pull the brakes on my life and take the time to question my direction. There were a thousand voices telling me that it was stupid to lower the pace, that I had to do everything right now when the doors were open, and that it would in no way be certain that great opportunities would be waiting for me if I pulled back for a whole season. But God was reminding me that He was in control, and that I had time to rest. So like Jeremiah went ahead and buried the deed of a property he had just bought, trusting that he would one day be able to return to it and harvest the fruits of the land, so I would now bury my newly earned degree and my opportunities for ministry, clinging to the hope that I would one day be allowed to return to them. In other words, I chose rest, trusting that I could depend on God to open new doors for me on the other side of this next season.

A SINGLENESS SEMINAR
July 2023

Back in March, I had committed to hosting a singleness seminar at a Christian youth camp. For a long time, I had felt a strong need to redeem some of the stigma that seemed to surround seasons of singleness. Maybe it was something I felt the need to do for my own process as well, but I figured this would be a good way to take a stance. However, at the time I agreed to host it, I had been dating someone, and now it felt like scratching in an open wound to prepare for the seminar. My heart was broken, and I wasn't thriving in singleness, so what did I even have to pass on to anyone else?

I was almost calling it off, thinking it would be too painful for me when a friend encouraged me to give it some extra thought. My emotions were very valid, real, and loud right now, but God had placed that idea on my heart for a reason, and I wanted to follow His lead, even in difficult circumstances. I ended up doing it, and I was so happy that I did.

Standing there, in front of a full classroom, God's truth about singleness just started flowing out of me in a way that felt more natural than it ever did before. I was not on the top of the mountain. I hadn't conquered the contentment of singleness. I was right there in the process with my audience, preaching God's truth and redemption over them as well as over myself. And I discovered something along the way: I really enjoyed teaching.

Afterwards, several people told me how great it was to hear this teaching from someone, who was actually single, herself. And then one girl came up to me and told me that this seminar had been an answer to her prayers. That I had put into words a lot of things that had been rumbling in her heart and helped her make sense of them. That was everything I could have hoped to achieve with my seminar, and I was beyond grateful that God would use me to bring healing and restoration to others in this area.

SETBACK
August 2023

With a heavy heart, I packed up my apartment and said goodbye to my life in the city that had been my home for the last five years. Even though I hadn't been doing well there for a long time, there were still a lot of amazing memories. The hardest part was leaving my church behind. These people had become an extended family for me to lean on and learn from in my first years of living on my own and growing into a young woman of God. I would never take for granted all the good things that had been sown into me within this community.

I moved back to my parents' place for a few weeks before school would start, and a full wave of defeat hit me. It felt like a huge setback for me to go to Bible college now. I was 25 and everywhere around me, people were getting engaged, married, having kids, and so on, while I had nothing going on for me. I was no longer a youth leader. I was no longer a part of any local church fellowship. I was no longer a master's degree student. It felt like I had been stripped of all labels that had given me a sense of status, and it felt terrifying, because who was I now? Just a nobody?

My older sister would be getting married in a few weeks, and my younger sister and her husband had just bought a car with space for a stroller. I so longed to be able to keep up with them, and it had seemed as though I finally closed in on them earlier this year, but it had slipped far beyond my reach again. My life was forcing me in a different direction, and there was nothing I could do about it. A factor that heavily affirmed this reality, was the fact that all the money in my children's savings account would be used for financing my stay at the school. Both of my sisters had used this money from our parents to finance their weddings, and I had left the money untouched all these years for the same purpose. In a weird sense, spending this money to pay for the school felt like stripping myself of the prospect of marriage in any near future, and it weighed heavy on my heart to do so.

I found some comfort in the story of Joseph. His life was marked with several setbacks, and every time things started to look great for him, it seemed there was another pit waiting for him to fall into. But God was there, and God was in control. Where Joseph perceived a setback, God was orchestrating a setup for leading him into his destiny. I wanted to trust that God could do the same for me in the middle of my setback.

GREEN PASTURES
August 2023

I really didn't want to go to Bible college. It felt more like a hopeless last option to me than it felt like a new adventure, and until the very last day before the school started, I looked for other things to do instead. But the day arrived, and my dad and I packed my things in the car and drove towards the school in silence. I pretended to be asleep to avoid any conversation with my dad. I knew that if he would begin asking me questions, I would not be able to hold back my tears, and I didn't want to arrive all red-eyed and messy.

A few hours' drive later, we arrived at the school, and I got the key to my room. I was happily surprised to learn that I would be living in a cozy room in the loft, from where I had an amazing view towards the forest and the fjord. It felt like God was welcoming me, a weary traveler, to this place of rest and restoration, and the whole situation seemed to communicate that "*now all will be well.*"

After a few days of introductions, new friends, laughter, and activities, I had a hard time remembering why I had ever felt such resistance towards coming to the school. It quickly became clear to me that this was the very best place I could possibly be in this season of my life. I got to have people around me all the time, I had plenty of time to read books and immerse myself in my theology studies, and best of all, I got to just be Line without any responsibilities at all. No one expected me to be a leader or to engage in ministry.

In many ways, it was a fresh start, and one day while I was lying in a hammock outside on a sunny afternoon, I realized that this was the manifestation of the Bible verse, where David writes "*He makes me lie down in green pastures. He leads me besides still waters.*" God was indeed a good Shepherd, and He hadn't failed in leading me to a place where I could find everything that I so desperately needed after a very heavy season.

SORROW AND JOY

August 2023

Only a week after school started, I went home again for my older sister's wedding. In all honesty, I didn't really want to go home and miss out of all the fun of introduction week. Further, my new community was already so much better for my well-being than home, which only reminded me of the hardships of the last many months. I felt bad about having these feelings, because my sister deserved for me to be present and happy on her behalf on one of the biggest days of her life. I wished that my current circumstances and my disappointed feelings didn't muddy my participation in her celebration.

The day turned out very well. My sister was so beautiful and happy, and her groom was in every way the kind of man I always wished for her to end up with. The church, in which they got married, was the same church, in which my younger sister and her husband got married two years earlier, and in more than one way there were some parallels between their stories. Both of my sisters found their husbands in the area where we grew up, and both of them dreamt about moving back there again, where they would have our parents and their in-laws around them.

This day, - her wedding day - felt in many ways like an answer to a prayer I had prayed for her as I had seen how much she longed for marriage and a family in the years where we had both watched our little sister enter into that chapter without us. Now my older sister was entering the marriage chapter as well, and I was the last one standing. I had a sense that my story would not follow theirs. My vision for life and for marriage didn't seem to fit within the walls of our childhood church. I didn't belong there, and it would feel like settling, if I suddenly did. At the same time, though, it made me feel incredibly lonely that the rest of my family had something in common that I didn't fit into. It's a difficult feeling to explain, but it hit me when I watched my dad walk down that exact same isle with the second of my two sisters.

The pastor mentioned in his speech that my sister was a person, who was definitely worth building a life with. I was happy that she had found a man, who heard these words from the pastor's mouth and felt the same in his heart of heart. And at the same time, it ripped at my heart, because I only had the experience of someone, who quickly didn't find me worth it. Would I ever find that? As they both gave each other their "yes" and placed the rings on each other's fingers, I wondered if anyone would ever adorn my hand with a ring.

After the ceremony, they signed their marriage contract, and my sister could now sign it with a new last name. Now I no longer shared my last name with any of my sisters, and again I wondered if anyone would ever change my last name to his own.

At the party later in the day, there were many great speeches. I was moved by how much my sister's in-laws loved her already, and how they celebrated her love for my new brother-in-law as well. And at the same time, it tore at my heart, because I so longed to experience this for myself. The most beautiful speech was given by the groom, and my heart exploded when I heard him express his love for my beloved sister. Tears began streaming down my face, but they were not only happy tears. Witnessing a love that had grown and grown all the way to the altar was such a contrast to anything I knew. Disappointment and longing hit me again right there in the middle of a crowded room, and I just considered myself lucky that everyone else thought they were tears of joy.

Sorrow and joy can live in the same heart. Sometimes our joy of seeing God blessing our friends and family with something is followed along by heavier feelings of what we still have to long and wait for in our own life. Joy is not contaminated by being accompanied by grief. Although being opposites, they can definitely coexist.

WALKING ON WATER
August 2023

Growing up, I was never the kid, who enjoyed getting dirty. I was always more of an indoor girl and to the great irritation of my sisters, I often preferred a quiet moment with a book to sports and outdoor games. In many ways though, it was a control thing. I always excelled in areas where I could use my mind, but it wasn't as easy for me to do well in areas of physical endeavors. I didn't like throwing myself into activities where I would either fail or be mediocre. So I often sat on the sideline in my life, when sports or other physical activities were on the program. This way, I got to stay in control, but it was accompanied by the unpleasant feeling that all my friends in the field were having more fun than me. The price I paid for control was my joy.

When I came to the school, I knew I wanted to challenge myself in this area. After many years of studying and after having been too grown up for too long, I was now more than ready to give myself permission to play and engage in activities where I didn't necessarily excel. The Bible college had a sports and adventure elective and on our first day, we went to a beach to do a full-body workout there. It was certainly a baptism by fire, but I was determined to give up control, and I did all the exercises with the biggest smile on my face, because I discovered something along the way: there is tremendous joy to be found in surrendering control. To not think about doing well. To not think about looking great. To not think about what other people think of you. To not think about the consequences of doing somersaults directly in the sand or running full speed into the water. And when I afterwards sat in the sand next to my new friends and looked at the water, tired and with sunkissed cheeks, I felt a deep sense of joy that had been gone for so long.

A few days later, God spoke to me through something as odd as my slippers. At the school, we usually walked around in slippers, and I had brought with me my old H2O sandals that I hadn't worn for years. But now I walked around in them every day, and I realized that I was quite literally walking on water in this season. I felt assured that I was on the right course here. Finally, I was on the adventure with God that I had been praying for, for so long. God was working on my joy and freedom right now. I got to break up with control in my life and play around like a little kid again, and it was soothing for my soul like nothing I had ever experienced before.

A TRAJECTORY ON GRIEF
August 2023

It was an incredibly healing experience for me to be at the school. We were still in that initial phase of the year where all the people were interesting and exciting, and we had yet to see each other's sins and flaws. Moreover, there were lots of programs, routines, and interruptions to prevent me from falling back into unpleasant thoughts and feelings.

Nonetheless, it didn't take more than a little time alone in my room one afternoon, before I was suddenly very heartbroken again after several days where everything had been alright. Was I healing here, or was I simply distracted? My sister told me that healing from grief is a tricky thing. We expect it to be a linear process - that the pain grows smaller and smaller, until we are finally whole again. In reality, though, it is more circular. In the beginning, you keep returning to the grief all the time, and it's not so much that it grows smaller over time, but more that you can go longer distances without returning to it, until one day when you no longer need to return at all.

GOD FOLLOWS YOU ON SOME

I am such a Pinterest girl. I love looking at images of beautiful things, and I love reading quotes from people, who managed to put my inner experiences into relatable words. So obviously, I have plenty of boards on my Pinterest, and one of them, I simply chose to call DREAMS. Here, I pin all the pictures and quotes that hit close to the core of my heart, though I cannot always put into words the dream that they represent to me.

One day in September, as I was scrolling through my DREAM board, I saw a number of images capturing beautiful desk setups in front of windows with a great view. The images would contain handwritten notebooks, candles, and flowers, and it signaled creativity, immersion, and beauty. Then it occurred to me that these images were something I was living out right now. My room at the school had a desk right in front of the window, from which there was an amazing view towards the fjord. I had decorated the desk with a pretty lamp, candles, and flowers, and further I had plenty of time in this season to sit there and read good books, take notes, study the Bible, and journal my thoughts and experiences.

God had given me one of the small dreams I had in my heart, without me even being able to explain, exactly what it was about. I was overwhelmed by how well He knew me, and how He had led me to a place where I could live out a dream that only my Pinterest bore witness to. God knew the dreams of my heart, and He gladly wanted to surprise me with something that brought me joy. The experience made me more confident that God knew exactly what He was doing. While He was still orchestrating the bigger things in my life, He didn't fail in giving me small reminders of how intimately He knew and loved me.

GIVING THANKS FOR THE BS

September 2023

The peaceful sanctuary I had built around myself at the school would not stay uninterrupted for long. One night, a girl at the school pulled me aside and told me that she just wanted to let me know how she had recently started seeing a guy and found out that he and I had been dating earlier in the year. Now she wanted me to hear it from them, before everyone else would find out about it. This news pulled the rug out from underneath me. It wasn't right for me to protest or anything, but it was just incredibly painful. The worst part was that I genuinely liked this girl, and I had thought that she would become a good friend of mine during my stay. A few weeks earlier, we had gone on a hike together and shared stories from our lives, and I had told her about some of the heartbreak and struggles that had been leading up to my coming to the school. Now I just felt hurt and betrayed after having shared such vulnerable things with her, and I couldn't even blame her, because she hadn't done anything wrong. She was just a girl, who had met a guy that she wanted to get to know better.

This whole situation led me down some less-than-pretty paths that I would have preferred to be without. One of the very natural paths that I took was that of comparison. This girl was just… shining. On all parameters, she radiated health, joy, and confidence, and I knew very well that I couldn't keep up with her in anything right now. She was everything that I had burned out trying to be, and she made it all look so effortless. And now she was also admired by the guy that I had wanted to be with. In some weird sense it felt like she walked on stage and took over my role in the future life I dreamt of for myself, just shining and twirling in all the spotlight, and receiving all the applause from the crowd, while I had been pushed to the shadows of behind the scenes - forced to passively watch it all.

Another path I took was one of bitterness. When you are the one who gets your heart broken, there is this strange sense of justice you want to achieve in at least being the first one to find something better for you. And although it rarely works out that way, it made me feel angry that it was so easy for him to replace me within the course of only a few months, while I was still licking my wounds, trying to just be okay again.

Yet another path I took was one of shame. I was being hurt so much by the actions of two people, who didn't do anything wrong, so I didn't think I even had the right to my emotions. It felt horrible to know that my broken heart made me an inconvenience to the guy, who had meant so much to me. Involuntarily, I had been forced into the middle of the arena in which his new love story was unfolding, as if I were the antagonist, whom the hero had to tip-toe around or fight off in order to be with his princess. It was a narrative that crushed me, when I still longed to be the main character in his life.

One good thing came out of all of this, though. It all helped me move on faster than I would have been able to on my own. God had gifted me with a tremendous amount of loyalty, but the other side of the coin to this valuable gift was that I tended to hold on for too long. With very loving intents, it felt like God was making the thing I held on to so incredibly hurtful that it forced me to let go in a hurry and move on to whatever God would have for me instead in this season.

ON BEEING SEEN
October 2023

On a Wednesday in October, we had an exercise in our prayer class. We simply had to close our eyes and ask Jesus where He was standing in the room with us. I saw Him standing in the other end of the room from my corner seat with plenty of people sitting between us. He told me "*I see you, Line*" and caught eye contact with me, and every time the people between us would move and block the way, he would adjust a little so He could still see me and look me in the eyes. Tears traced silent paths down my cheeks as Jesus was doing his healing work in letting me know that I wasn't overlooked by Him in all the hardships of the past weeks.

I was never someone, who wanted to be the center of attention, but I hated when I was being overlooked or disregarded, just because I wasn't drawing attention to myself or raising my voice to get what I wanted. And lately, it had just felt like all the louder people in my life, and those with sharper elbows and more charisma got ahead and received God's blessings, while I was still just stuck in the background. I wondered if Joseph ever felt overlooked in prison when he saw other people's dreams come true, while his own dreams were still unfulfilled after years and years of waiting.

At least I felt overlooked, and I began wondering if there was something wrong with my approach. But then Jesus stepped in and let me know that He saw me. He saw me even though I preferred the corner seat. He saw me even though I would never yell across the room. He saw me exactly as I was, and He wouldn't want me to change anything to get His attention or His blessings. He simply saw me, and He hadn't forgotten me in His good plans.

A KINDRED SPIRIT
November 2023

There was one person at the school, who had quickly become one of my favorite people to spend time with. It was so easy to be around him, and conversation always flowed naturally and effortlessly between us. He seemed to feel the same way about me, so we often ended up in each other's company. In many ways, he was very different from me, but I found him incredibly interesting to listen to and talk with, and I loved the way he was able to make me laugh and drag me out of my shell to become myself more authentically.

Lately, though, I had been a little bit concerned about this newfound friendship. I didn't usually invest in friendships with guys, and now, as he became more important to me, I had no internal code of conduct for how to navigate a friendship like this. From the beginning of the school year, he had been very clear about the fact that marriage was not in the plans for his life, and as I very much wanted to marry my best friend, I had a feeling that I needed to set some boundaries to protect my heart. Though all these reservations rumbled in the back of my mind, I still threw myself into the unknown waters of this connection, as I had found something very rare to me: a kindred spirit.

On a random Saturday, as it had happened so many times before, we found ourselves in the library, sitting in each our armchair and talking. Our conversations often spanned from surface level everyday stuff to the very deep topics, and this day was no different. I didn't know how we did it, but we went from discussing our tastes in Christmas decorations to go look through the old yearbooks in the archive section of the library. He told me how both his parents and his grandparents had met each other at the school. Something here made me curious, and as our conversation flowed past our respective families, I asked him about his own prospects of family. To my surprise, he gave me a very honest answer. *God was doing something.* And although he didn't want to tell me, I had a feeling that it had something to do with me.

During the next weeks, something shifted within me. In my mind, I wondered if this friendship had potential for more by some crazy miracle that God had been orchestrating without my knowing it. As I talked to Jesus about my friend, I recognized in him more and more of the qualities I had been praying for in a future spouse. My stomach suddenly fluttered with butterflies. I found myself becoming flustered and nervous around him, and I asked myself what it meant when we sat next to each other and our arms and legs brushed against each other without any of us moving. Did he feel the same way about me, or did I read it all wrong?

Relationships can be faith journeys too, and it felt very much like I was on the brinks of embarking on a big one here. I no longer had a fixed idea of what my future would look like, so I couldn't tell if he would fit into it, and that scared me. I knew that it would not be an easy road for any of us, if we went ahead and pursued this journey together, and frankly, I was too scared to get my heart broken again. But I thought I saw God's hand at work in all of it, and I wanted to take the risk of going where He would lead me, so I told God that if this was truly from Him, then my friend, and not I, would have to pursue the relationship by initiating the talk of how we felt about each other.

WHEN HISTORY REPEATS ITSELF
March 2024

"*Not again*" was the first and only thing that came out of my mouth, when I stood in his room and recovered from the initial chock of his rejection. Not again. This last half year had been incredibly healing, but in no way did I yet have the strength to go through another dark valley of heartbreak.

Shortly before Christmas, we had found out that we had feelings for each other, and even though we were both uncertain of how to move forward from there, there was a tremendous joy in knowing that we shared something special like that. We spent more intentional time together during the next couple of months, and one day at the end of January, it occurred to me that a year had gone by and now once again, I found myself sitting in a café, drinking hot chocolate, and getting to know someone. Only, this time around, it felt so much better, because it was within the safe frames of a friendship. However, ghosts of the past have a tendency to show up eventually, and when he started talking about future, and it seemed like our lives could go in different directions after summer, I felt a wave of anxiety creep into my heart. Was this him trying to pull away? Did our relationship have a termination point already? Would I be enough to be considered worth the distance this time around? Weirdly enough, I felt peace in the fact that I was. It was so clear to me that he genuinely liked me. We had our rough patches, and a lot of uncertainty surrounded us as we moved forward, but I felt confident that we cared enough about each other that we would face the challenges together.

But now, here I was again. In a painfully ironic way, the timing of it all seemed like history was repeating itself, and I just couldn't believe that I would have to go through the same thing again when this friendship had felt so much like God's redemption. Never had I expected that he would rather lose me than proceed on this challenging journey with me by his side. I had been certain that I truly meant a lot to him, and I couldn't understand how he could just let go of someone that he cared for so much. I knew that it hadn't been an easy process for him, but I couldn't deal with the fact that a part of him perceived me as a threat to be pushed to an arm's length when what I wanted the most was to be his safe place. It completely broke my heart.

For the first time in my life, I had actually fallen in love – not with an idea of someone that would fit well into a future I saw for myself – but I had simply fallen in love with exactly who someone was. And now I didn't know what to do with all that love. I think it's one of the worst feelings in the world, holding something so pure and powerful in your heart for someone, and in the blink of a moment they can turn into such an imposition, what was never meant to be anything but good and right.

I wanted to beg him to fight for me and for us, but something stopped me - maybe the fear of being so vulnerable with him when I knew with certainty that it would be followed by a rejection. The only thing that I could do was to bury myself in his arms, trying to postpone the moment that I would walk out of his room, because I knew that from the minute I did, nothing would ever be the same between us again. And I just wasn't ready to let him go.

ANOTHER EASTER ANALOGY
April 2024

The Saturday must have been the hardest part of Easter for everyone except Jesus, I would imagine. The Saturday is the horrible "in-between" day – this dreadful leap of faith between the letting go of your former dreams and plans and the getting to see what God had in mind instead. It's the day of nothingness, of waiting around, and of mind-blowing fear that God might not come through for you.

When my friend went ahead and killed "us", people advised me to bury the whole thing properly to make myself ready for whatever God would have for me instead. This was good advice. I would have given most of my friends the same advice. But for some reason, I just couldn't do it. I wanted to be able to give him my friendship instead, although I was unsure if I would even be able to. I didn't want to get hurt and clobbered and lose my authenticity in denying my feelings for him. But if he couldn't give me more, and I couldn't give him my friendship, then the only thing left was to become strangers again, and that prospect was just too painful. In a weird sense, it felt like saying that it didn't mean anything and that everything – the friendship as well - could and should just be forgotten. And that was simply not true, because it had meant so very much to me. For that reason, I chose to swallow all the pain that came with suppressing my own wants and needs to at least attempt staying friends with him. I simply couldn't bury us.

The theme of burial, however, covered more than just one area of my life at the moment. I had given myself permission to rest until Easter without trying to plan my future, but now I would have to start thinking about what I would want to do after summer. I had received a few different ministry proposals, but I felt hesitant in all of it. It seemed that everyone would expect me to just continue in the same direction as before I came to the school, but in reality, this season had foundationally altered my priorities, and I couldn't tell if that was a good thing or not. As I was sharing these thoughts with a group of friends, someone reminded me of the story of Abraham, who was asked to give up his son, Isac. I knew God was asking me to let my calling die. I had built up so much control around predicting outcomes, trying to live up to other people's expectations and limiting my calling around a very specific way of doing ministry, and now God was telling me to bury it all, because He knew best. In His timing, not mine, He would resurrect it.

I really needed to hear this, and I went home and wrote the following in my journal:

I needed permission to not try to seek control. I needed permission to just be still and wait on God instead of seeking and finding solutions. I needed permission to not walk the beaten track. Permission to not do what is perfect. Permission to live a life where the equation doesn't seem to balance. Permission to not use all of the talents I have been given at one and the same time. I think that something I have learned and keep learning here at the school is that I have a role to play in just being me. I don't have to take on a role of leadership to make a difference. Maybe I actually make more of a difference without a lot of responsibilities. This feels like a paradigm shift. Moving from control to faith. And that is what I prayed about for so long - a life of adventure with you, Jesus! So now when my bank account is completely drained, and my future is uncertain, it is exactly me living the life I used to only dream about living. It looks foolish in other people's eyes. And it isn't the belief system my family lives by, nor the one I have been raised to live by. It doesn't rationally make sense. But it is complete surrender.

So you can have my fancy business degree and my church leadership program, Jesus! It doesn't mean anything either way, and sometimes it feels more like a burden than something good. You can have my future - all my plans, dreams, and hopes. You know better than I!

INCREASING INTIMACY
May 2024

One of the goals I had for this year at the school was to grow in the prophetic. I knew that great adventures with God was also about following the lead of His voice in my everyday life. One day, we had a seminar on the prophetic, and our teacher told us to just ask God what He might want to tell us in that moment. Immediately, I heard Him tell me that He thought I was brave. And then He told me that He was proud of me. In all the weariness of stepping out on uncertain paths, these words felt amazing. God didn't call me stupid, naive, or irresponsible. He called me brave. He was proud of me for stepping out of the boat and trust Him to make a way for me, whether it would end in disappointment or not.

Towards the end of April, we had a retreat week at the school, which allowed us to spend more scheduled one-on-one time with God. I started every day in my room, asking God what He wanted to tell me and then wrote down what I thought I heard Him say to me. This was where I realized something profound: Hearing God's voice was way simpler than I had made it into. I found out that it had a lot to do with belief.

Did I believe God was a good Father? *Yes.*

Did I believe that a good Father would speak to His children? *Yes.*

Could I generally believe that when I asked Him something, the answer I heard in my mind would be His reply to me? *Yes.*

So I started journaling with God. I wrote with a black pen, and I gave Him a purple one. I would tell Him about my state of mind and write down His comforting replies. I would ask him a question, and He would give me an answer.

And then a second revelation hit me. Greater intimacy with God was not about reaching a point where everything else in life became less important. It was more about inviting Him into all of it and process everything with

Him, from the big identity questions to the small everyday experiences. I loved this newfound way of communicating with Him. I would sneak away during the day and spend time with Him, and I would ask Him what He wanted to tell me, and in faith I would write down, what I heard Him say. Sometimes it made sense and came straight out of the Bible. Sometimes it didn't, and I would have to ask Him some clarifying questions to make sense of it. And sometimes again, I got it wrong, and that was okay. He let me know that we were learning to communicate in a new way.

This level of intimacy with God was one I had been praying for since my boarding school years more than a decade ago. At that time, I had wanted that intimacy to happen from one day to another, but now I saw why maybe God hadn't answered my prayer in that way. Years and years of daily Bible reading had made me well aware of what my Shepherd's voice sounded like, and I was now able to steward this level of communication in a way I would have never been at that time. Sometimes, God takes us on a longer road, before He gives us the blessing, but He knows what He is doing. It's always far worth the wait.

A STURDY STEPPINGSTONE
June 2024

When it was time for me to leave the school, I didn't feel quite ready for it. Even though I had known all along that my time here was temporary - just a steppingstone to whatever came next - it had grown on me and taken up my whole heart. This place had become home, the people had become family, and the routines had become my whole life. This year had been everything I needed and so much more, and it felt heavy having to accept that life moved on, and I would have to do the same. Especially when, once again, I had to exchange something very good with a future I couldn't yet see.

All I knew was that I would be moving to Aarhus with three girls I had gotten to know at the school. Everything else was still uncertain. I felt at peace in my decision, though. I knew my thriving would still very much depend on having people close to me every day, so in a myriad of possibilities, that was what I chose to move for. I wanted to trust that God would have a great plan for all the other areas of my life as well, but I knew I had to close this chapter first in order to find out what it was.

One of the things I brought with me from this amazing year was a major break with religion. I had been so used to living my life within the walls of principles, rules, and rigid blueprints of how to navigate different scenarios in life, but during this year, I had found something so much better: The guidance of the Holy Spirit. The life with the Spirit wasn't the safe choice – I still had a broken heart to testify to that. It came with no guarantees of avoiding failure or falling into pits along the way, but it came with the promise that He would be there with me every step of the way. Further, I found a deep joy and freedom in breaking the walls of religion, cutting all the strings of control, and allowing myself to be childlike, led by my good Shepherd, and in constant awe of what surprises He might have for me around the next bend on the road. This was the adventure I had been longing for all my life, and not before God had stripped me of all my former idols and aspirations, had I been able to find it. Even despite the painful aches of my heart, I could testify that He had truly been good to me this year.

LIVE WHAT YOU LEARNED
July 2024

When being back home at my parents' place for the summer, I was trying to determine, how to make ends meet for my next year. I really wanted to finish my bachelor's in theology in order to graduate with a large group of friends next summer. However, this would cost me a lot of money that I would have to save up by working. With a well-paid job, I would maybe be able to work part time and thus have time for my studies. But a well-paid job would require more of my mental capacity, and that would ruin the joy of studying and leave me stressed out. With a less well-paid job, I would have to work more hours to pay my expenses, leaving no time for my studies. I just couldn't find a great solution, and I was no longer willing to press through at the expense of my own well-being, so the only thing left to do was to drag out my studies over the course of two years instead of one. I was sad to let go of the prospect of graduating with my friends, but on the other hand, I was proud of myself for standing firm on what I had learned during this year of rest. I would no longer try to do everything at once. I would rather give myself permission to have the time and energy needed to fully enjoy and be present in all areas of my life.

SUMMERTIME SADNESS
July 2024

New summer, new battle was what I noted down in my journal in a moment of frustration. There were a lot of unpleasant emotions connected to moving back home with my parents for another summer. It was the first summer that I was there on my own, as my sisters were settled and busy with each their schedules, and I was constantly comparing my own journey to theirs. My youngest sister and her husband would soon be welcoming their first child into the world, - something that would give my parents the title of grandparents for the first time. I, on the other hand, had just borrowed a great amount of money from my parents to even be able to pay for the deposit to my new apartment. I was painfully aware of the difference between these two events, and I was blaming myself for my situation in life – a circumstance that was in many ways way beyond my control.

It was always a constant ambivalence, though. On the one hand, I couldn't picture myself living the lives of my family. It felt too predictable, and I knew I would be settling for less, if my life would suddenly look like that. I wanted the adventure, and I was happy that my journey looked different. On the other hand, I longed for connection and having the comfort of building life with someone long-term. I hoped very much that my story would become a "both and", and not an "either or". That I would get to have plenty of adventures AND get to experience the comfort of a family. I turned to Jesus with all my frustrated feelings, and I knew that He wanted me to trust Him with my timeline and my journey. He let me know that He was writing a good story over my life. The best stories have drama, plot twists, points of no return, and moments of despair, and I felt comforted that this season was only one chapter with many more to come.

ISLAND LIVING
August 2024

It was an adventure moving into our new home. Our apartment was placed on a peninsula close to the waterfront, and I could even see the ocean from the window in my room. The weather in August was amazing, and we would often go for swims during the days or in the evenings. One early morning, I went out to watch the sunrise at the water's edge, and on another day, I went to the other side of the island to watch the sunset between the masts of all the boats. The whole environment on the island made me feel comforted somehow, and I loved that God had provided me with a home in this season, around which He had placed small reminders of His promises. The harbor with all the boats was His reminder to me that He was my safe haven in this season. Nothing was too big or too small for me to bring to Him. The lighthouses around the island were His reminder to me, that abiding in His light would make me a ray of light in other people's lives. The waterside was His reminder of the invitation to go deeper into the journey of faith adventures with Him, and the rocks along the pier reminded me to go crab fishing with my friends and allow myself to experience the moments of childlike wonder.

I was also thrilled to experience God's provision in blessing me with not just one, but three amazing roommates for this season. I remembered back to my time before Bible college where I thought my youth was over and it was too late for me to have the experience of living with good friends, and I was amazed by how God had proved me wrong. Nothing is ever too late when God is in the picture, and He knows exactly how to orchestrate our journeys so that we get to live out old dreams that we may have given up on a little too soon.

THE TIMING OF TRANSITIONS
September 2024

Only a week after I moved in, I received a phone call with a job offer that would mean that I had to move to another part of the country. A number of things made me suspect that this could be God calling me, so I told the person on the phone to keep me posted on the position.

First of all, I knew that God's timing for calling us out on faith adventures wouldn't always fit perfectly with our schedules, and this did indeed feel like a bad sense of timing. The last time I received one of these radical invitations, I would have had to give up an apartment, which I had just moved into, had I chosen to follow Him out on the depths.

Secondly, this job looked like a steppingstone to what God and people had spoken into my life over the past few years. Though the tasks of the job appeared slightly mundane, it seemed like a strategically wise step for me to take into my future.

Thirdly, I quickly realized that this move would bring me closer to a friend I deeply missed, and I wondered if God somehow had a plan with this. At least, I found it worth exploring.

Lastly, God had spoken over this particular year that I would take bigger steps of faith in my journey with Him, and this was indeed a BIG one that seemed to fit with that narrative.

Although I wanted to follow God's calling, I was also frustrated with the whole thing. While a part of me was excited for the adventures ahead, another part of me grieved the fact that I would now have another season in front of me that would only be very temporary. How did I invest here in this city, when I knew I was on my way in maybe only half a year's time? How could I let down my roommates already and say goodbye to this living arrangement that I had been so happy about? It felt unfair somehow, but I wanted to believe that God had led me in this direction for the time being, and that this season wouldn't be wasted, even though He cut it short. Maybe it was gracious of Him to give me knowledge about my next steps already, so I would know not to bind myself too tightly to anything here.

BIG CITY LIFE
October 2024

It was an old dream of mine coming true to be living in a big, vibrant city for a season. Big city life comes with grand opportunities for spontaneity, social get-togethers and exploration of new areas that leads to discovery of small hidden gems, and I was all here for it in this season of my life.

Although my heart was still hurting, and my mind was partly set on the new adventures ahead, I wanted to stay present and build memories with the people I was living life with right now, so it made me happy when in September, we jumped on our bikes and had a bonfire on the beach south of the city. It was one of those great evenings where the sky was colored with the prettiest palettes, and we enjoyed each other's company, while making s'mores and singing worship songs until it was completely dark, and we could see the lights from the city skyline reflect in the water. A friend and I stayed there for the night and slept in the sand under the open sky, and though it was cold and uncomfortable, it made our hearts very happy.

In October, one of my friends came by to go to a Taylor Swift event at a night club in the center of the city. I spontaneously decided to join, and we danced for several hours straight, drowning all of our problems in the lyrics that we screamed out loud on the dance floor. I had never been much of a dancer. Although I genuinely loved to dance, I always ruined the joy of it, because I got way too self-conscious about it. But this night, I really had the time of my life. When we walked home from the event, I told my friend how this experience had felt like redemption. I could tell that I had grown to become more free and joyful, and I loved it from the bottom of my heart.

A POLISHED ARROW

October 2024

On a random day in October, I asked God for an image, and all I got was an image of an arrow accompanied by the words "*a polished arrow*". I didn't take it seriously, but I felt God urge me to write it down, even though I didn't see any direct application. We were practicing, and He wanted me to trust Him with the mysteries as well. I wrote down the word and made a Google search on it, and then I found out that it was actually written in the Bible!

In Isaiah 49 it read "*he made me a polished arrow; in his quiver he hid me away.*" I asked God what He wanted to tell me with the word, and He told me that this was a season where He was making me a polished arrow. He was working in areas of my life that would prepare me for what was ahead. But this was also a season of being kept in His quiver. In other words, He wanted to keep me hidden from the spotlights of ministry, but I could trust that He was still at work in my life.

I felt relieved. Upon my moving, I had been trying to figure out how I wanted to serve in church, but truth be told, I couldn't find the motivation to enter church ministry again, and it didn't make it easier for me in the setting of a new, big-city church. In the back of my mind, I knew it was expected of me to re-enter ministry, and it made me feel guilty and frustrated that I hesitated and didn't seem to be able to find my place. But God's voice should always be louder in my life than the voices of others, and I found my peace in knowing what His expectations were for me in this season.

HOW HEALING COMES ABOUT
November 2024

Sharing an apartment with three other people came with more challenges than I expected. It wasn't that I walked into it blindly. I had expected conflicts to arise when we would try to combine four different views on what made up a home. I even welcomed it, because I wanted to grow in my skills of living life closely with other people – conflicts and everything. What I didn't expect, though, was the magnitude of it, and how much introspection it would bring along for me.

I found, that when a conflict arose in our home, my reaction was to become invisible. I shoved down my needs, stayed in my room, and tip-toed around everyone, trying not to fan the flames. When I was asked to voice my opinion on matters of conflict, I stubbornly refused for the same reason. I wanted peace more than anything, and that seemed to be the one thing I couldn't achieve, no matter how much I tried to mediate and not take up any space for myself.

At the same time, this whole atmosphere brought up to the surface old memories from my childhood home. I realized that my reaction patterns had been similar then, until I decided to move out at the age of 20 and hadn't dealt with it since. I suspect God often brings about change in our lives like this, though. He allows us to revisit old patterns in order to lead us to healing and transformation, and that was exactly what was happening here. I began to understand that I couldn't live my life by shutting down or running away every time I found myself in the middle of a conflict.

In relation to this, my mom came to me one day and initiated a conversation about some reaction patterns she had noticed in me when we gathered as a family. She listened to my experiences and made sure to let me know that she wanted me to feel like I had a space in our family. To be honest, I had given up the hope of ever having these kinds of emotionally honest conversations with my mom, so for this conversation to take place without my doing anything was so clearly the grace of God at work in my life. It healed some parts of me that had been hurting more than I cared to admit.

God, in his infinite wisdom, used my circumstances in this season to bring about healing in an area of my life where I wouldn't have even known where to begin the work myself. That's what God can do, and I was blown away by His greatness in orchestrating the timing of it all.

DEAD-END STREET
November 2024

In November, I visited the town that I was planning to move to, but the stay didn't turn out the way I expected at all. On my way there, I randomly met an acquaintance of mine, and we started talking. It's weird how you sometimes run into very specific people at very significant moments. It's almost as though God planned it out. I told him about my thoughts on moving, and in response, he found it wise to share some news with me—news that, at that point, he was one of the only people in my social circle able to share. It felt like an emotional bomb had been dropped on me, but I knew that my plans of moving had to be based on rationality or faith – not on my emotions.

We continued our conversation and got to talk about family. While he was very eager to have one, I was more hesitant in voicing my dreams in this area. Family would be a great blessing, but to me it didn't feel like something that I could just choose to pursue. I knew it had to be done God's way or not at all. He mentioned something about my focus on career, and that made me uncomfortable. Suddenly, I saw this move in a whole new light, and I wasn't sure that I liked what I saw. What was really important enough for me to want to move across the country for it? I didn't want my career to be the answer to that question. Truthfully, the more I thought about it, the more I was afraid that I had somehow disguised myself in some holy imagination and narrative about a big calling, because it hurt too much to admit my longing for a family. Focusing on my career seemed like something that was at least partly within my control, whereas the dream of a husband and a family felt well beyond my sphere of control.

After my job interview later that day, I walked around in the town with tears streaming down my face, and I felt a deep sense of loneliness in the prospect of moving there. This was not the place for me, and all I wanted was to jump on a train and go back home to my apartment, where I could be allowed to break down and hide from the world. So that was what I did, and my roomies were ready with duvets, snacks, and Christmas movies. A few days later, I turned down the job offer.

In the following days, I had some heavy reactions to all of it. I felt awful about changing my mind so rapidly on something in which I had only expressed certainty for a long time. I didn't want to be someone you couldn't rely on. These feelings reminded me of the very similar situation from only a few years ago where I turned down a ministry opportunity and went to Bible college instead, and it made me feel like a big failure that I now twice in my life backed out of an opportunity for ministry due to my emotional volatility. On the one hand, I was afraid of burning my bridges and on the other hand, I didn't care much about it. I somehow knew that I wanted to take a different path, anyways.

I had been scared to admit it, but with the help of good questions asked by my traveling companion that day, I eventually reached the conclusion that relationships were the most important thing to me. This was ultimately what I wanted to move across the country for, and why would I ever do that when all my friends and family were right where I was now? I became aware as well that I wanted to live my life in a slower pace – a life with an open home and a present heart. And I wanted to make space in my life for creativity – I wanted to allow myself the time and space to create for the joy of doing it. So after a few days of processing everything, hidden away in my beloved home, I finally began the process of writing this book.

BUILDING BOUNDARIES
December 2024

For some time, God had been talking to me about boundaries. A few times during the fall, I had literally had dreams where I would scream at people for doing something that was not okay, and it always felt good to let all of my emotions out. Now, this was of course not a constructive way to deal with other people's BS in waking life, but the essence of it all was my ability to stand up for myself, and that felt incredibly empowering.

I knew that God placed a lot of value on me, and I wanted to align myself with His truth and allow myself to take up more space in my own life. I wanted to allow myself to speak up about what I wanted for my home. I wanted to allow myself to take the time I needed to process different options and to change my mind - and change it again if I needed to. I wanted to allow myself to disappoint other people with a *"no"* whenever there was something I didn't feel like doing. I wanted to allow myself to ask from people what I truly wanted, even if rejection and disappointment was at stake. I wanted to give myself permission to take risks in going after my wildest dreams and not care about anyone else's opinion, but God's. I wanted to own my own journey and not be conformed to anyone else's idea of what made up a "good" or "successful" life.

WHERE DO I BELONG?

January 2025

I had applied for 75 different jobs during the last half year, and after I finally went on my very first job interview in the beginning of January, and I didn't get the job, I completely broke down in exhaustion. At this point, I was so tired of the whole process of getting my hopes up about a job, just to have them shattered again by a formal e-mail, explaining that they found someone better suited for the task.

For half a year now, I had made ends meet with the money I got paid from my unemployment insurance, but this money wasn't only not enough to pay my bills in the long run – it was also attached with all the stigma of not working for your own paycheck. I wanted to find a part-time job so I could still find time for social life and studies, but there weren't a lot of part-time jobs out there. Further, I had to spend time applying for two full-time positions every week that I knew I didn't even want to have, just because these were the rules of the insurance company. When I applied for the jobs I actually wanted, it felt like my resume was standing in my way. With entry-level jobs, I wasn't taken seriously, because of my age and my master's degree. With vocational jobs, I didn't have enough specialized experience, because I had spent all my time in church instead of taking on more business-related jobs.

More than ever before, I just felt like I was being caught between two worlds, struggling to be taken seriously by anyone, because I had chosen both instead of one over the other. On the one hand, I felt the expectations for me to pursue a fulltime high-paced job to kickstart my career in the business world. On the other hand, I felt the expectations to not let my calling to ministry fall through the cracks. I felt stuck in the middle, unsure of what I actually wanted to do, and I desperately knocked on every single door within reach, but nothing opened up.

I felt weary and confused from changing my mind daily, trying to adapt to every new opportunity I would pursue, in my attempts to get out of my current state of unemployment. I knew that God in His greatness could give me a job in the glimpse of a moment, but I didn't understand why it hadn't happened yet. In the end, I just wanted to give up altogether, and in the wasteland of waiting around, I was overwhelmed with a frustrating feeling of not having a place anywhere.

The day I got the rejection phone call about the job I had interviewed for, I vented to my roommate and later that day, she sent me a series of pictures that she had drawn, accompanied by the following text:

When you are feeling tired and overwhelmed,

and you feel like you don't know where you belong,

don't forget that your place is here with us,

and more importantly, your place was, is, will be here in the hands of God.

I was moved to tears when I read through the images. She was right. I did have a place, and I would have to regain my trust in God for Him to provide me with the right job at the right time. Once again, I surrendered my timeline and found peace in the fact that this was a time to finish my book and spend time with my beautiful roommates. Meanwhile, He wouldn't fail in opening new doors for me to walk through.

HANDING OVER THE PEN

January 2025

A few months ago, my dad sent me an article about the woman that my home street is named after. Apparently, she was a female writer, and I kind of liked the thought of walking in her footsteps right now. It served as another sweet neighborhood reminder from God of what He wanted me to do in this season. Although the dream of writing a book had been there for many years, and God had already given me the green light almost a year ago, I now finally gave myself permission to immerse myself in writing it. The words flowed out of me – forming on the pages the words, phrases, and descriptions that had already been built up in my head.

Looking back on these years of my life, now well-documented within the pages of this book, I realized that I have grown in many ways. I have learned that growth often looks like unbecoming layers of what is not authentically you in order to reach the core underneath. I have learned that even when life pulls the rug out from underneath you, and you feel like you have reached the end, there are always new and better paths to follow. I have learned that letting go of precious dreams and hopes in tears, eventually will lead to resurrections of joy. The processes were messy and painful, but also thrilling and exhilarating.

I believe this is the perfect time to end my book. At the age of 26, it feels like I am still in the middle of exploring, learning and becoming, and I haven't yet reached any real destinations. Not that we ever really get to reach definite destinations in this life, and not that I would want to settle in any kind of destination mindset. I want to be on the move with God, and I am excited about wrapping up this chapter and moving on to the next. I feel optimistic about the future and about the hidden adventures waiting down many yet unknown paths.

One main thing I have learned in the process of writing this book is that growth has a lot to do with surrendering control. I have had a bad habit of writing my own chapter endings to my story, but I have also learned that God is a much better writer of stories than I am. The story we read in our Bible is proof of this. So I made a deal with God that I would stick to writing about events that have already happened, and for what comes next, I will hand over the pen. I will trust the Author of life to write a good story with mine.